Science Fair
Projects

S e r i e

D0753793

Botany:

49 Science Fair Projects

Robert L. Bonnet and G. Daniel Keen

TAB BOOKS

Blue Ridge Summit, PA

This book is dedicated to Shannon Bonnet.

FIRST EDITION
FIFTH PRINTING

© 1989 by **TAB Books**.
TAB Books is a division of McGraw-Hill, Inc.

Library of Congress Cataloging-in-Publication Data

Bonnet, Robert L.
    Botany : 49 science fair projects / by Robert L. Bonnet and G.
  Daniel Keen.
       p.   cm.
    Includes index.
    ISBN 0-8306-9277-0   ISBN 0-8306-3277-8 (pbk.)
    1. Botany—Experiments. 2. Botany—Exhibitions.   3. Science
  projects. I. Keen, G. Daniel. II. Title.
  QK52.6.B66   1989   89-34644
  581′.078—dc20   CIP

TAB Books offers software for sale. For information and a catalog, please contact TAB Software Department, Blue Ridge Summit, PA 17294-0850.

Acquisitions Editor: Kimberly Tabor
Technical Editor: Lori Flaherty
Director of Production: Katherine G. Brown

Other Books in the
Science Fair Project Series

EARTH SCIENCE:
49 Science Fair Projects (No. 3287)

This second volume in the series concentrates on Earth's geology, meteorology, and oceanography, as well as the Earth's crust, weather, solar energy, acid rain, fossils, and rocks and minerals.

ENVIRONMENTAL SCIENCE:
49 Science Fair Projects (No. 3369)

This third volume in the series deals with Earth's surroundings and how pollution, waste disposal, irrigation, errosion and heat, and light affect the ecology.

About the Authors

Robert Bonnet holds an MA degree in environmental education and has been teaching science at the junior high school level in Dennisville, New Jersey for more than 15 years. He is also a State Naturalist at Belleplain State Forest in New Jersey. During the last seven years he has organized and judged many science fair projects, at both the local and regional levels. Bonnet is currently the chairman of the Science Curriculum Committee for the Dennisville School system.

Daniel Keen holds an Associate in Science Degree, majoring in electronic technology. He is a computer consultant who has written many articles for computer magazines and trade journals since 1979. Keen is coauthor of two books published by TAB BOOKS Inc., *Mastering the Tandy 2000* and *Assembly Language Programming For The TRS-80 Model 16*. In 1986 and 1987, he taught computer science at Stockton State College in New Jersey. His consulting work includes writing software for small businesses and teaching adult education classes on computers.

Together, Bonnet and Keen have published articles on a variety of science topics.

Disclaimer

Adult supervision is advised when working with these projects. No responsibility is implied or taken for anyone who sustains injuries as a result of using the materials or ideas put forward in this book. Taste nothing. Use proper equipment (gloves, safety glasses, and other safety precautions). Clean up broken glass with a dust pan and brush. Use chemicals with extra care. Wash hands after project work is done. Tie up loose hair and clothing. Follow step-by-step procedures; avoid short cuts. Never work alone. Remember, adult supervision is advised. Safety precautions are addressed in the text. If you use common sense and make safety the first consideration, you will create safe, fun, educational, and rewarding projects.

Contents

Acknowledgments

The authors wish to extend their appreciation to the following people:

George M. Keen; photography and editorial assistance.
Victor Gilson; Chief School Administrator, Dennis Township School.
Carl Gallela; Principal, Dennis Township School.
Tom Keck; Superintendent, Belleplain State Forest.
John D. Webersinn; Webersinn's Landscaping.

Introduction

At some time during our school years, all of us have been required to do at least one science project. It might have been growing seeds in kindergarten or building a Telsa coil in high school, but such experiences are not forgotten and help shape our views of the world around us.

Doing a science project yields many benefits beyond the obvious educational value. The logical process required helps encourage clear, concise thinking which can be carried throughout a student's entire life. Science in general requires a discipline of the mind, clear notes and data gathering, curiosity and patience, an honesty of results and procedures, and last, a concise reporting of work accomplished. A successful science project might provide a student with the motivation to strive for success in other areas.

Often, parents are encouraged to work with their children on projects, thus fostering richer family relationships, as well as enhancing a child's self-esteem.

Finally, there is always the possibility of a spin off interest developing. For instance, a child who chooses to do a project in mathematics, perhaps using a battery, switches, and light bulbs to represent binary numbers, might discover a liking for electronics.

But where does the student, teacher, or parent find suggestions for such projects? It is our aim to remedy this void by offering a large collection of projects and project ideas in a series of books. These books target anyone who wants or needs to do a science project. A teacher might want to do classroom projects. A student might be assigned to do a class project by a science teacher, or to enter a project in a science fair. A parent might want to help their child with a science fair project. A person might want to do an experiment or project just for the fun of it. Science teachers can use these books to help them conduct a science fair at their school or to suggest criteria for judging. Parents might feel apprehensive when their child comes home with a project requirement to do for school. These books will come to the rescue.

Our goal is to show you project ideas from beginning to end. Students need a starting place and direction. We have provided that with questions posed in the form of needs or problems (discovering how to get electricity from the sun was born out of a need, for example). We have also provided overviews, organizational direction, suggest possible hypotheses, indicated materials, procedures, and controls. The projects explained are complete, but can also be used as spring boards from which to create expanded projects. All projects are brainstormed for going further. The reader will be shown how to develop ideas and projects using valid scientific processes and procedures.

Each chapter is organized by topic. Some projects might overlap into more than one science discipline as well as within the discipline. We have attempted to place these projects under their dominant theme. You can quickly skim through the topics of interest and "home in" on a project suitable for a student's ability or interest level.

Projects are designed for the sixth to ninth grade student. Many projects, however, can be "watered down" and used for children in lower grades. Similarly, students in higher grades can brainstorm ideas to more advanced levels.

It is very important to read the introduction at the beginning of the chapter from which you plan to do a project. Information that is relevant to each project is given there. For example, in the chapter on hydroponics, each project shows a "nutrient solution" in the materials lists, but it is not explained. The chapter introduction, however, defines this term and gives procedures for creating it. In addition, the source list in the back of the book lists suppliers where nutrient solutions and other laboratory supplies can be purchased ready-made.

After you have selected a project and read the introduction, read the entire project through carefully. This will help you understand the overall scope of the project, the materials needed, the time requirements, and the procedure before you begin.

Safety and ethics must be a consideration before beginning any project. Some projects require using a knife or scissors. Use common sense. Projects that *must* have adult supervision are indicated with the phrase "Adult supervision required" next to the title. These projects deal with caustics, poisons, acids, high temperatures, high voltages, or other potentially hazardous conditions. Ethical science practices involve very careful consideration of living organisms. One cannot recklessly cause pain, damage, or death to any living organism.

There is no limit to the number of themes and the number of hypotheses about our universe. It is as infinite as the stars in the heavens. Hopefully, many students will be creative with the ideas presented, develop their own unique hypotheses, and proceed with their experiments using accepted scientific methods.

Some projects can go on for years. There is no reason to stop a project, other than getting tired of it. It might be that what you studied this year can be taken a step further next year. With each question or curiosity answered, more questions are raised. It is our experience that answers produce new and exciting questions. We believe that science discovery and advancement proceeds as much on excellent questions as it does on excellent answers.

We hope that we can stimulate the imagination and encourage creative thinking in students, teachers, and parents. Learning is rewarding and enjoyable. Best of luck with your project.

Robert L. Bonnet
G. Daniel Keen

1

Science
Projects

Before beginning work on a science project, there are some important things you need to know. It is important that you read this chapter before starting on a project. It defines terms and sets up guidelines that should be adhered to as work on your projects progresses.

Beginning Without Pain

To proceed with a science project, you must first fully understand the term "science project." Older students are familiar with report writing. Many types of reports are required at all grade levels, whether it be book reports, history reports, or term papers. Although a report might be required to accompany a science project, it is not the focal point, but experimentation. Most projects discover information by scientific methods. The scientific method is a formal approach to scientific investigation. It is a step-by-step logical thinking process and can be grouped into sections:

1. The statement of the problem

2. The hypothesis

3. Experimentation and information gathering (results)

4. A conclusion based on the hypothesis

In science, a statement of the "problem" does not necessarily mean that something went wrong. A problem is something for which there is no good answer. Air pollution is a problem. Aggressive behavior, crab grass, and obesity are problems. Any question can be stated as a problem.

Discuss your ideas with someone else, a friend, teacher, parent, or someone working in the field you will be investigating. Find out what has already been done on the subject and if the scope of your project is appropriate.

A hypothesis is an educated guess. It is educated because you have knowledge about trees, dogs, or whatever the subject matter of your project is. Your life experiences also help you form a specific hypothesis rather than a random one. Suppose you hypothesize, "If I add sugar to water and feed it to this plant, it will grow better." A "control" plant would be needed, namely, a plant that was given only water. Both plants would be given the identical amount of sunshine, water, temperature, and any other nonexperimental factors.

Assumptions

Any assumption in science must be defined specifically. What is meant by saying, "The plant will grow better"? What is better assumed to be? Does it mean greener leaves, faster growing, bigger foliage, better tasting fruit, more kernels per cob?

If you are growing plants from seeds, the assumption might be that all of the seeds are of equal quality. When several plants are used in an experiment, it is assumed that all the plants are the same at the start of the project.

Before beginning a project, be sure to state all of your assumptions. If the results of an experiment are challenged, the challenge should be on the assumptions and not on the procedure.

Sample Size

Sample size refers to the number of items in a test. The larger the sample size, the more significant the results. Using only two plants to test the sugar theory would not yield a lot of confidence in the results. One plant might have grown better than the other simply because some plants just grow better than others. Obviously, your statistical data becomes more meaningful the larger the group of items you use in the experiment. As the size increases, individual differences have less importance.

Making accurate measurements is a must. The experimenter must report the truth, and not let bias (his or her feelings) affect his measurements. As we mentioned earlier, the reason science progresses is because we do not have to reinvent the wheel. Science knowledge builds on what people have proven before us. It is important to document (record) the results. They must also be replicable (able to be repeated), so others can duplicate our efforts. Good controls, procedures, and clear record keeping are essential.

As information is gathered, the results can lead to further investigation or raise more questions that need asking.

The conclusion must be related to the hypothesis. Was the hypothesis correct or incorrect? Perhaps it was correct in one aspect but not in another. In the sugar example, adding sugar to the water might have helped, but only to a point. The human body can use a certain amount of sugar for energy, but too much could cause obesity.

There is no failure in a science experiment. The hypothesis might be proven wrong, but learning has still taken place; Information has been gained. Many experiments prove to be of seemingly no value, except that someone reading the results will not have to spend the time repeating the same experiment. This is why it is important to thoroughly report results. Mankind's knowledge builds upon success and failure.

Collections, Demonstrations, and Models

Competitive science fairs usually require experimentation. Collections and models by themselves are not experiments, although they can be turned into experiments. A collection is gathered data. Suppose a collection of shells has been assembled from the eastern seaboard of the United States. The structure and composition of shells from the south can be compared to those found in the north. Then the collection becomes more experimental. Similarly, an insect collection can deal with insect physiology or comparative anatomy. A rock and mineral collection might indicate that there is a greater supply of one type over another because of the geology of the area from where they were collected. Leaves could be gathered from trees to survey the available species of trees in your area.

Classroom assignments that use demonstrations or models can help students to better understand scientific concepts. A steam engine dramatically shows how heat is converted to steam and steam is converted into mechanical energy. Seeing it happen might have greater educational impact than merely talking about it.

Individuals Verses Group Projects

A teacher might want a group of students to work on a project, but groups can be difficult for a teacher to evaluate. Who did the most work? If, however, it is dealt with on an interest level, then the more help received, the better the project might be. Individual projects verses group projects bear directly on the intended goal. Keep in mind, however, that most science fairs do not accept group projects.

Choosing a Topic

Select a topic of interest; something that arouses curiosity. One only needs to look through a newspaper to find a contemporary topic: dolphins washing up on the beach, the effect of the ozone layer on plants, stream erosion.

Limitations and Precautions

Of course, safety must always be first when doing a project. Using voltages higher than those found in batteries have the potential for electrical shock. Poisons, acids, and caustics must be carefully monitored by an adult. Temperature extremes, both hot and cold, can cause harm. Sharp objects or objects that can shatter, such as glass, can be dangerous. Nothing in chemistry should be tasted. Combinations of chemicals might produce toxic materials. Safety goggles, aprons, heat gloves, rubber gloves for caustics and acids, vented hoods, and adult supervision are just some safety considerations. Each project should be evaluated for safety materials. Projects in this book that require adult supervision are indicated in the project title. Finally, special considerations should be considered if a project will be left unattended and accessible to the public.

Most science fairs have ethical rules and guidelines for live animals, especially vertebrates, which are given thoughtful consideration. In some cases, you could be required to present a note from a veterinarian or other professional that states that training with the animal has been dealt with. For example, using mice to run through a maze, demonstrating learning or behavior.

Limitations on time, help, and money are also important factors. How much money will be spent should be addressed by a science fair committee. Generally, when a project is entered in a science fair, the more money spent on the display, the better the chance of winning. It isn't fair that one child might only have $1.87 to spend on a project, while another might have $250. Unfortunately, at many science fairs, the packaging does influence the judging. An additional problem might be that one student's parent is a science teacher and another student's parents are unavailable or unable to help.

Science Fair Judging

In general, science fairs lack well defined standards. The criteria for evaluation may vary from school to school, area to area, and region to region. We would like to propose some goals for students and teachers to consider when judging.

A good project is one that requires creative thinking and investigation by the student. Record keeping, logical sequence, presentation, and originality are important points.

The thoroughness of a student's project reflects the background work that was done. If the student is present, a judge might orally quiz to see if the experimenter has sufficient understanding. Logging all experiences, such as talking to someone knowledgeable in the subject or reading material on it, will show the amount of research put into the project. Consequently, urge students to keep a record of all the time they spend on a project.

Clarity of the problem, assumptions, procedures, observations, and conclusions are important judging criteria as well. Be specific.

Points should be given for skill. Skills could be in computation, laboratory work, observation, measurement, construction and the like. Technical ability and workmanship are necessary to a good project.

Often, projects with flashy display boards do better. Some value should be placed on dramatic presentation, but it should not outweigh other important criteria such as originality. Graphs, tables, and other illustrations can be good visual aids to the interpretation of data. Photographs are especially important for projects where it is impossible to set the project up indoors (a "fairy ring" of mushrooms in the forest, for example).

Some science fairs might require a short abstract or synopsis in logical sequence. It should include purpose, assumptions, a hypothesis, materials, procedures, and conclusion.

Competition

Often a project will compete with others, whether it is at the class level or at a science fair. Find out ahead of time what the rules are for the competition. Check to see if there is a limit on project size. Will an accompanying research paper be required? Will it have to be orally defended? Will the exhibit have to be left unattended overnight? Leaving a $3,000 computer unattended overnight would be a big risk.

Find out which category has the greatest competition. You may be up against less competition by placing your project in another category. If it is a "crossover" project, you may wish to place it in a category that has fewer entries. For example, a project that deals with chloroplasts could be classified under botany or chemistry. A project dealing with the wavelength of light hitting a plant could be botany or physics.

Botany

This book deals with a wide range of ideas in the category of botany. Botany is the scientific study of the plant kingdom. Complete projects are shown. Many additional ideas for going further are brainstormed and are left for the reader to develop and investigate. Most of the equipment and supplies required for these projects are inexpensive items or items which can be found around the home. A resource list is given in the back of the book for supplies required for some projects, such as those in hydroponics where nutrient solutions are needed.

The projects presented here target children ages eight to thirteen. Many of the projects can be watered down for younger children and expanded for older students. Pick a project that is at your level of ability and narrow enough for you to accomplish. It should not require equipment or supplies beyond what can be obtained. For example, a project requiring lodgepole pine cones should not be attempted if these cones are not available.

We hope you get a good feeling of accomplishment as you delve into the fascinating world of botany.

2
New Plants from Old

Growing seeds makes excellent projects for all ages. A seed has enough stored energy to grow a stem and push it through the soil where a leaf can form. Indeed, it is not just good enough for the stem to break through the soil surface, a leaf and root must form in order to absorb additional energy from sunlight, water, and nutrients from the soil. If a seed is outdoors and it takes too long to germinate, the growing season can be missed.

Seeds have great importance to mankind. Essentially, every type of food we eat had its origin in some form of plant. The seed is the conclusion of a plant's life cycle (note that there are some plants that do not have seeds). Seeds ensure continued growth of a species.

Continuation of a species is called reproduction. There are two principle types of reproduction, sexual and asexual. Asexual is a form of reproduction that does not use special reproductive organs. The vegetative parts of an existing plant (roots, stems, leaves) are capable of making new plants by vegetative propagation. In complex plants, asexual reproduction includes rhizomes, tubers, corms and bulbs. These are naturally occurring. Artificial reproduction can be done by cutting, grafting, and budding. Seedless grapes are grafted from an original plant, which occurred by accident.

Sexual reproduction is the fusion of the nuclei of specialized cells to produce a zygote. The zygote is the new organism.

PROJECT 1
Don't Bury Me too Deep
(Adult Supervision Required)

Overview

A problem that exists naturally for seeds is that some get buried deeper than others, it depends on who buries them: man, the wind, birds, or perhaps a squirrel. Propose a hypothesis that some seeds might not produce plants if they are buried too deep.

Materials

- several clear, wide mouth jars or an aquarium
- large stones
- sand or gravel
- potting soil
- seeds, preferably radish, green bean, or corn
- black construction paper
- rubber band or tape
- ruler

Procedure

You will need several clear, wide mouth jars, or an aquarium. The aquarium does not have to be water tight, since we are not filling it with water. Fill the jars or aquarium with about an inch of large stones. Next, add a layer of sand or gravel. On top of these layers, put six or seven inches of potting soil (see Fig. 2-1). Potting soil is better than soil from your backyard because outside soil usually contains some wild seeds or other organisms. If you intend to use outside soil, have an adult bake it at 400 degrees for 15 minutes to kill most living organisms. The bottom layers under the soil help the water drain past the seeds. Draining reduces the possibility of seeds rotting.

Purchase some seeds at a seed store, preferably radish, green bean, or corn seeds because these grow fast and have good roots and stems. (Use only one of the seed species suggested.) Soak the seeds overnight in water. This helps break down the seed coat.

Plant some seeds on the surface of the soil, some about one inch down, some at two inches, and so on. Plant four or five at each level. Plant as many levels as your container allows. All of the seeds should be planted next to the outside wall of the jars or aquarium so you can see them.

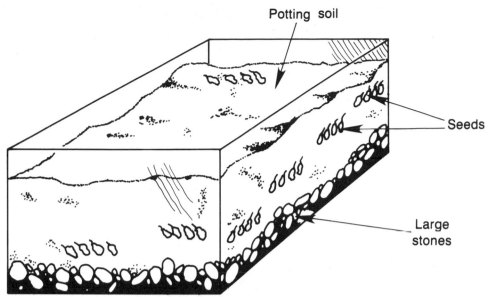

Fig. 2-1. Bury seeds at different levels to determine the effect of depth on germination.

Cover the jars or tank with black construction paper to keep the sunlight from shining on the seeds. Use a rubber band or tape to keep the paper in place. Each day, the paper will have to be removed for a few minutes while you observe the seeds' growth.

Keep the soil moist but be careful not to put too much water in the soil. Be sure to water all the soil evenly so all seeds get an equal amount of water. Also, if you are using jars, keep all of them in the same area so they are at the same temperature.

Make a log chart to record your daily observations, such as the one shown in Fig. 2-2. Include the date, and what each of the seeds is doing. Even if you see no change, be sure to write that information down too: Monday January 2. Nothing yet. When stems and roots appear, measure the length of each separately every day.

Conclude whether your hypothesis was correct.

Going Further

1. Is there a "faster" growth period? By that we mean is there a several day period when the plant grows more than at other times?

2. Hypothesize that seeds planted closest to the surface germinate faster.

3. Which produces more plants, seeds planted deeper or those planted near the surface? After six weeks of equal care, weigh the parts of the plants that appear above the ground.

Date	Surface Planted Seeds	Seeds Planted 1 inch	Seeds Planted 2 inches	Seeds Planted 3 inches	Seeds Planted 4 inches

Fig. 2-2. Sample log for recording *Don't Bury me too Deep* data.

PROJECT 2
Hot Seeds

Overview

Does temperature affect germination? Is germination slowed by cold? Will it be speeded up by increased temperature? Is there a particular temperature that will produce the best results?

There are three types of seeds we can test. The first type has two cotyledons with no endosperm (sunflowers and peas). The second type has two cotyledons with endosperm (castor bean). The third type has one cotyledon plus endosperm (corn, wheat, rice, millet, rye).

Materials

- 4 two-liter plastic bottles with the top cut off
- 4 thermometers
- topsoil
- 12 sunflower seeds, 12 castor bean seeds, and 12 corn seeds
- ruler
- black construction paper
- tape

Procedure

Put soil into each of the four containers, about three inches from the top. Plant three seeds from each species in a group in each container. (Bury seeds at the same depth and close to the side.) Cover the outside with a piece of dark paper. There should be three groups (with three seeds per group) in each of the four containers (see Fig. 2-3). Use the tape to mark the seed locations (Fig. 2-4). Throughout the project keep the seeds moist at all times.

Place a thermometer in each container. Then put one container in a very cold place (such as a cellar floor or inside a refrigerator). Place another in a very warm place (such as direct sunlight on a sun porch or the top of a refrigerator toward the back). Place another in a moderately cool place. Read each thermometer three times a day. Turn the containers one-third of a rotation each day to prevent one set of seeds from receiving more heat or cold from the environment. Record observations in a log such as the chart shown in Fig. 2-5. What is happening? Have any seeds germinated?

Water only enough to moisten the seeds. Use room temperature water, not directly from the tap. Do not take your readings within the hour

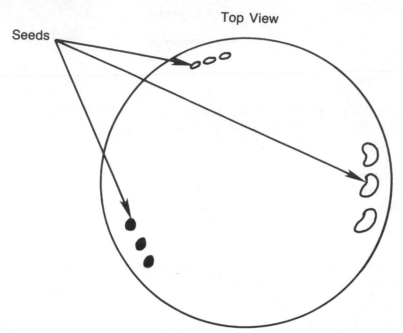

Fig. 2-3. Top view of seed container before top layer of soil is added.

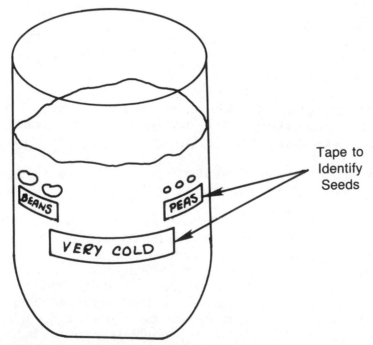

Fig. 2-4. Side view of seed container. Use tape to identify seed types and locations.

DATE	Very Cold Observation			Moderately Cold Observation			Moderately Warm Observation			Very Warm Observation		
	BEAN	CORN	SUNF	TEMP	BEAN	CORN	SUNF	TEMP	BEAN	CORN	SUNF	TEMP
date												
AM												
noon												
PM												
date												
AM												
noon												
PM												
date												
AM												
noon												
PM												

Fig. 2-5. Sample log for recording *Hot Seeds* data.

of watering. The water may cause a temperature change. Open the paper to make an observation only once per day. Continue the project until leaves form. Conclude whether or not your hypothesis was correct or not.

Going Further

1. The information gathered might show the seed opening early at one temperature, but root growth faster at another temperature.

2. Is one temperature better for one seed species and another temperature better for a different species?

PROJECT 3
Home Is very Important
(Adult Supervision Required)

Overview

In nature, seeds are found in various soil environments. Different soils percolate (drain) water at different rates. Some soils will hold moisture longer than others. Water percolates (drains) quickly through sandy loam soil, leaving it quite dry. Seeds can germinate in several different types of soil. Some seeds can only live in one type of soil. Planting several different kinds of seeds in several different types of soil, hypothesize that all the seeds will not germinate and grow at the same rate.

Materials

- watermelon, sunflower, and green bean seeds
- potting soil
- sand (such as that used in sandboxes for children)
- three containers with drain holes in the bottom (3-liter plastic soda bottles, margarine tubs, or large diameter flower pots)
  Note: Have an adult drill or punch holes in the bottom of the plastic containers.
- masking tape or labels
- ruler

Procedure

Fill one container with potting soil, one with sand, and the third with one-half potting soil and one-half sand. The containers should have holes in the bottom to let water drain out. Plant three or four seeds of each type about one inch from the surface of the soil. Label the container for soil type and seed position (see Fig. 2-7).

Place the containers in a warm area (about 70 degrees Fahrenheit) but not in the direct sunlight. Give each group of seeds an equal amount of water, about three ounces every day. Observe their growth and keep a log as suggested in Fig. 2-6. Define the term germination to mean the time it takes for a plant to emerge from the seed until a stem first pushes above the soil and leaves appear. Did sunflowers grow at the same rate in all of the soil types? Did green beans? Watermelons?

Date	Jar #1 Sand	Jar #2 Potting Soil	Jar #3 50/50 Mixture

Fig. 2-6. Sample log for recording *Home Is Very Important* data.

Fig. 2-7. Fill one container with potting soil, one with sand, and one with half soil and half sand. Plant seeds in each.

Going Further

1. Add humus to the potting soil and test.

2. Add nitrate to the sand and test.

3. In the fifty/fifty mixture, try different ratios of sand to potting soil such as ¾ potting soil to ¼ sand.

PROJECT 4
Take a Bath

Overview

Seed coats are a protective outside covering on a seed. These coats must be opened allowing space to grow for the infant plant inside. In nature, some seeds are exposed to stomach acids when animals swallow them. Other seeds are opened by tumbling along shallow streams. Still others are buried in soil near the roots of trees where the soil might have acids (tannin). Some seeds soak themselves open. In all cases, the outer protective covering must be broken before it can continue to grow. Will seed soaking reduce the total germination time?

Materials

- 12 green bean seeds
- 12 radish seeds
- 12 watermelon seeds
- 3 containers
- potting soil
- 9 paper cups

Procedure

Label the paper cups "Green beans one hour," "Green beans eight hours," and "Green beans 24 hours." Do the same for radish and watermelon. Label the larger container one hour, eight hours, and 24 hours. On the side, label radish, green beans, and watermelon, equally spaced as shown in Fig. 2-8.

Begin the experiment at 6:00 p.m. Place four seeds of each seed type in their 24 hour cups. Cover with luke warm tap water. Store at room temperature. On the next day, at 10:00 a.m., set up the eight hour cups. Use four seeds per cup. Cover with luke warm tap water. Place them with the others. Last, at 5:00 p.m., use the remaining four seeds of each species to set up the one hour cups. Store with the others.

Prepare the three containers with potting soil. At 6:00 p.m., take the seeds from their soaking cups and bury them at the same depth, placing all the 24 hour seeds in one container. Do the same for the eight hour seeds in another container, and the one hour seeds in the last container. Cover them and keep them moist. Use the chart shown in Fig. 2-9 to record your observations. Indicate which seeds show through the soil's surface first. Did you hypothesize correctly?

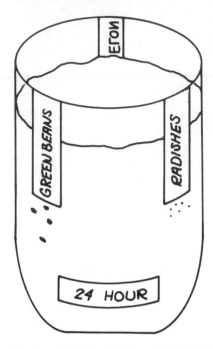

Fig. 2-8. Label three containers to indicate where radish, green bean, and watermelon seeds are placed. Label one container "1 hour," one "8 hours," and one "24 hours."

Date	Green Beans			Radishes			Watermelon		
	1 hour	8 hour	24 hour	1 hour	8 hour	24 hour	1 hour	8 hour	24 hour

Fig. 2-9. Sample log for recording *Take A Bath* data.

Going Further

1. What is the optimum soaking time beyond which no decrease in germination time is observed.

2. Use tea (tannic acid) and lemon juice (citric acid), as a soaking solution and compare it to water soaking.

3. Will nutrients aid in breaking down the seed coat? Use dissolved plant food in the water.

PROJECT 5
Rip Van Winkle

Overview

Most seeds require a certain amount of time after leaving the fruit before they will germinate. If a seed is taken out of a tomato, will it start growing immediately if it is planted? How long, if at all, does a tomato seed have to lie dormant before it can germinate? Is there a maximum time period beyond which a seed will not germinate? Can dormancy periods be artificially shortened?

Materials

- 8 airtight sandwich bags (Zip Lock)
- 6 dozen tomato seeds (from fresh tomatoes)
- 6 dozen sunflower seeds (picked from a sunflower)
- 6 dozen cucumber seeds (taken from a fresh cucumber)
- 6 dozen watermelon seeds (picked from fresh watermelons)
- potting soil
- containers
- freezer
- paper towels

Procedure

Gather the fresh fruit and remove the seeds. Rinse them off to remove any material on them. Dry them out on paper towels. When thoroughly dry, seal them in plastic storage bags. Half of the seeds will be kept in the freezer and half in a dark location at room temperature. All must be kept dry in sealed bags.

Plant four of each seed type immediately. These seeds will have no time to be dormant. Keep the seeds moist and see if they germinate.

Once each month, remove four seeds of each type from the freezer, and plant them. Also remove four seeds of each from the room temperature bags and plant them. Label all containers.

Use a log like the one shown in Fig. 2-10 to record and compare observations.

This project will answer the hypothesis that seeds require a dormancy period. It will also yield us much information about the normal dormancy period of each vegetable species and tell us if dormancy periods can be altered by making the seeds believe a winter season has passed.

| | Month #1 | | Month #2 | | Month #3 | | Month #4 | | Month #5 | | Month #6 | | Month #7 | | Month #8 | |
	room temp	frzr temp	room temp	frzr temp	room temp	frzr temp	room temp	frzr temp	room temp	frzr temp	room temp	frzr temp	room temp	frzr temp	room temp	frzr temp
Tomato																
Water- melon																
Cucumber																
Sun- flower																

Fig. 2-10. Sample log for recording *Rip Van Winkle* data.

Going Further

1. How long will seeds remain viable (able to germinate and grow)? This research could go on over a period of several years.

2. Will heat (say, 120 degrees Fahrenheit) allow the seeds to germinate either with freezing or without?

3. Can a seed's dormancy period be overcome if we have an over abundance of oxygen? How about an over abundance of carbon dioxide? What effect does temperature have on dormancy?

4. Will soaking or scarification (scratching the seed coat) permit germination before normal dormancy time?

3
Photosynthesis

Have you ever picked up a piece of plywood that has been sitting on the ground and noticed that the patch of grass underneath has lost its green color? Without sunlight, chlorophyll departs from the leaves since it is unused and photosynthesis cannot take place.

Photosynthesis is the process whereby green plants produce food and release free oxygen. To do this, plants need carbon dioxide (CO_2), water, sunlight, chlorophyll, and small amounts of minerals. Experiments in photosynthesis can involve varying any of these requirements, temperature, introducing pollutants, or trauma to the plant.

PROJECT 1
In the Dark

Overview

The leaf is the part of the green plant that does the chemical work of photosynthesis. It takes in carbon dioxide CO_2 and sunlight. Water is transported from the root system in the presence of a special compound, chlorophyll, the leaf can make food. How would covering one leaf of several leaves affect the plant? Will it cause the plant to produce more or bigger leaves? Will the plant become less healthy?

Materials

- 4 healthy indoor or outdoor plants, (each must have five or more leaves)
- 2 or 3 square feet of dark plastic (from a garbage or lawn bag)
- masking tape
- ruler

Procedure

Count the number of healthy leaves on each plant. Determine if they are of a similar size. A good method would be to count them in pairs. The largest with the smallest; the second largest with the second smallest, and so on. The middle group would be the average size. Measure the average-sized leaves (two or three pairs) and calculate the total area of leaf surface. Cover the middle or average pair with the dark plastic. Be sure to poke some holes in the underside of the plastic to allow air to flow in and out while restricting light.

Calculate the percentage of surface cover and write it on the tape. Place it on, or near, the plant container. Set up the second, third, and fourth plants with different covered areas. Be sure to identify each plant with the percentage of covered area (see the chart in Fig. 3-1 and the illustration in Fig. 3-2 as an example).

Each plant must receive the same amount of sunlight, water, and temperature. The only difference will be the amount of leaf surface exposed to sunlight.

Observe the overall condition of the plants. Determine whether one plant forms more or new leaves faster.

This entire project can be accomplished with outdoor plants, but be sure they receive the same identical conditions.

Conclude whether your hypothesis was correct based on the results.

Date	Plant #1 ____% covered	Plant #2 ____% covered	Plant #3 ____% covered	Plant #4 ____% covered

Fig. 3-1. Sample log for recording *In the Dark* data.

Going Further

1. Experiment using different colored plastics. Clear plastic, such as sandwich wrap, would make an excellent transparent cover.

2. Plants grow from the most recent growth. Test this hypothesis by covering one plant entirely, except for the two lowest leaves, and totally cover another except for the top two or three leaves.

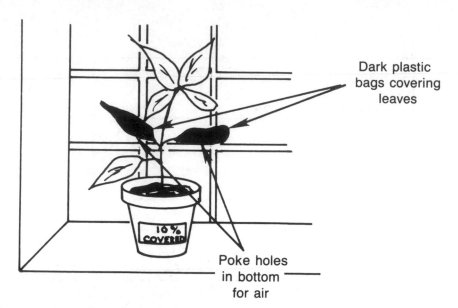

Dark plastic
bags covering
leaves

10%
COVERED

Poke holes
in bottom
for air

Fig. 3-2. Cover several leaves of the test plants. Use pieces cut from dark plastic bags. Poke holes in the bottom to allow access to air.

PROJECT 2
The Ides of Starch
(Adult Supervision Required)

Overview

The photosynthetic process of plants produces sugar, which is stored as starch. Does this process happen during the day or night? Is it ongoing and continuous? Is the starch found in the leaf, stem, or root?

Materials

- 1 house plant with green leaves and several green stems
- iodine (Note: iodine is poisonous if ingested)
- slice of white bread
- slice of raw potato
- 5 small dishes
- eye dropper

Procedure

Place a slice of potato on a dish. On another plate, place a slice of bread (see Fig. 3-3). Put five or six drops of iodine on each. Observe the color change. It should turn black or blue, showing the presence of starch. Next, take a piece of leaf, a piece of stem, and a section of the plant's root. Place them on separate dishes. Be sure to put the iodine on the open, exposed part of each piece. Is there a color change indicating the presence of starch? If starch is present, it should turn blue or black as the bread and potato did. Record your results.

Conclude whether your hypothesis was correct based on the results of your experiments.

Going Further

1. Use a healthy plant with several stems and many leaves. Examine for starch in the stem, leaf, and root parts during the late afternoon on a sunny day. Perform the same tests after 24 hours or more of darkness. Record your results and compare. Was starch present in all parts in both tests?

2. Is there a method to quantify the starch that is present?

Fig. 3-3. Put four or five drops of iodine on a slice of bread and on a slice of potato to test for starch.

Slice of potato

PROJECT 3
Color Me Red
(Adult Supervision Required)

Overview

Visible light comes in many wavelengths and is broken up into the colors of the spectrum—red, orange, yellow, green, blue, indigo, and violet. Colors outside of the visible spectrum, which cannot be seen with the naked eye, are infrared, which comes before red, and ultraviolet, which comes after violet.

Infrared lamps, ultraviolet lamps, and colored cellophane change the type of light a plant receives. Colored cellophane restricts the same color of light entering. Consequently, if you use blue cellophane, blue light is filtered out. Red cellophane restricts red light.

Does the type of light a plant receive affect how it will grow? Hypothesize that both ends outside of the visible spectrum of light will produce greater plant growth.

Materials

- infrared lamp and ultraviolet lamp or colored cellophane
- 4 or 5 healthy plants (each with five or more leaves)

Procedure

Before you begin: Ultraviolet and infrared lamps can be very dangerous and should only be used with adult supervision. Ultraviolet light can damage the retina of your eye. Infrared lamps produce much heat and can cause serious burns. Always wear safety glasses with an ultraviolet lamp and **never look directly into the ultraviolet lamp**.

Begin all of the plants at the same temperature, the same soil, and amount of water. Put all of the plants on a watering schedule. Place two control plants in regular, direct sunlight.

If you are going to use cellophane, put the test plant in the sunlight with the colored cellophane filtering out a particular color, such as yellow, blue, or red. If you are using an ultraviolet lamp, set it up so that it strikes only the test plant. Do not let sunlight hit the plant during the experiment. Turn on the lamp during the daylight hours and filter the light when sunlight is hitting the plant. Remember, **do not look into the ultraviolet lamp**.

Place the other test plant near the infrared lamp, but be sure not to put it too close to the plant because it gets very hot. Filter out sunlight so that it does not hit the plant.

Observe and record the results in a chart such as the one shown in Fig. 3-4. Conclude whether your hypothesis was correct based on the results of your experiment.

Going Further

1. Form an hypothesis that using different colored cellophane on one day, and another on the next day, and alternating every other day for several weeks, will yield better growth.

2. Do plants use different wavelengths of light at different points in their growth process? Will ultraviolet light help plants to flower, bear fruit, or germinate? What about infrared light? Will it help in these different processes?

Date	Control plant	Plant #1 infrared covered	Plant #2 ultra-violet	Plant #3 green filter	Plant #4 blue filter

Fig. 3-4. Sample log for recording *Color Me Red* data.

PROJECT 4
Autumn
(Adult Supervision Required)

Overview

Chlorophyll is a catalyst (helper of a chemical reaction) that enables plants to make food in the photosynthetic process. Chlorophyll is a green pigmented substance that is present in all green growing things.

In this experiment, we will measure the quantity of chlorophyll in leaves that have been given different quantities of light to find out if the amount of chlorophyll increases, decreases, or remains the same.

Materials

- 3 or 4 healthy house plants (each with five or more leaves)
- alcohol
- small piece of cardboard
- several sheets of paper
- 3 test tubes
- test tube holder or glove
- measuring cup
- stove

Procedure

Set up the plants in a well lighted area. Control all other factors: temperature, soil conditions, and watering. Each plant will be removed from the sunlight at a different time. Begin shielding (or removing) plants at different intervals. Remove the first plant from light and mark down the day. Two days later, remove the second plant from the light and mark it down. Two days later, remove the third plant from light and mark it down. The following day, run all of the experiments. You will have a plant marked "5 days shielded," one marked "3 days shielded," and one marked "1 day shielded."

To check for chlorophyll, cut a section of leaf from each plant. To quantify (to measure the amount) of chlorophyll in each shielded plant, use the same amount of leaf material. Select a size that is appropriate to the leaves you are using. It might be a one-inch square. Cut out a one-inch square from a piece of cardboard and mark each of the three healthy leaves that you cut. Keep them on pieces of paper marked with their plant number, or shielded time.

Set up the double boiler as shown in Fig. 3-5. Fill the pot with water and the test tube with alcohol. Use approximately four ounces of alcohol in each test. Caution: *alcohol is very flammable*. Do not use a high flame to boil the water.

With adult supervision, boil the water in the pot. When the water begins to boil, turn down the heat just to maintain the boiling condition. Use the least amount of heat to keep the water boiling.

Place the test tube with the leaf and alcohol in the boiling water. Bring the alcohol to a boil. Boil the alcohol for 10 minutes.

Next, begin your second specimen, following the same safety precautions. Complete by doing the third specimen. Evaluate the containers.

Conclude whether or not your hypothesis was correct based on the results of your experiments.

Going Further

1. Test leaves that recently fell from trees and compare with leaves that are still on the trees. Use leaves of a comparable area.

2. Is there more chlorophyll per unit mass in pine trees or in deciduous trees?

3. Compare cross sections of the two types of leaves. Evaluate the palisade and spongy layers, which layers contain the chlorophyll.

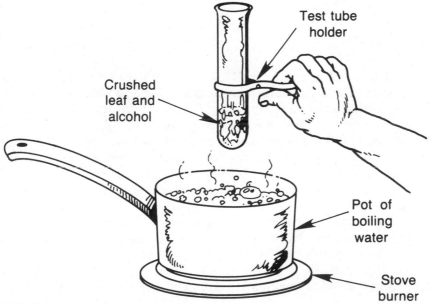

Fig. 3-5. Use tongs for added safety.

PROJECT 5
Hold Your Breath
(Adult Supervision Required)

Overview

Plants breathe by taking in carbon dioxide. On the underside of deciduous leaves are small openings called stomata. Stomata takes in whatever is in the air. Therefore, if the air is polluted by smokestacks, car exhaust, or other pollutants, the organism (trees or plants) will take them in. In fact, in New York, Maine, and some of the New England states, there are many tracts of trees suffering from air pollution.

In this experiment we will block a plants stomata causing it to hold its breath, much like air pollution does, to determine if it will contain less chlorophyll.

Materials

- petroleum jelly
- 5 healthy house plants (each of equal size and species)
- alcohol
- double boiler
- small piece of cardboard
- scissors
- 2 test tubes
- test tube holder or glove
- stove
- measuring cup

Procedure

You will need five healthy house plants, two of which will be controls. Since we are experimenting only with carbon dioxide, soil, temperature, and water must remain equal in all plants.

Coat the underside of a leaf on one plant with petroleum jelly as shown in Fig. 3-6. This will prevent the stomata openings from receiving air. The plant will not be able to breathe. Two days later, shield another leaf of a different plant by coating the underside with petroleum jelly. After another two days, coat a third plant with petroleum jelly.

The following day, remove the coated leaves from the three plants and one leaf from each of the control plants. Cut a square area from the cardboard. Using the cardboard as a template, cut out an equal area in size from each leaf.

Always observe the condition of the leaf before you cut it because it can have an affect on the experiment. Does one look greener, healthier, browning, curling? Record all of your observations.

As shown in Fig. 3-7 fill a double boiler with water and set it aside on the stove burner. Fill the test tube with about four ounces of alcohol and the uncoated leaves. Bring the water to a boil, but do not use a high flame.

Once the water is boiling, turn down the heat, but keep the water boiling. Using tongs or gloves, place the test tube in boiling water. Bring the alcohol to a boil. Boil for about 10 minutes then remove from heat. Remember, alcohol is very flammable, be extra cautious and always use tongs or gloves.

When the test tube has cooled, set it aside and open it to let the alcohol evaporate, leaving only the chlorophyll—the green pigmented substance.

Use the same procedure for the leaves coated with petroleum jelly then compare the chlorophyll. Was your hypothesis correct?

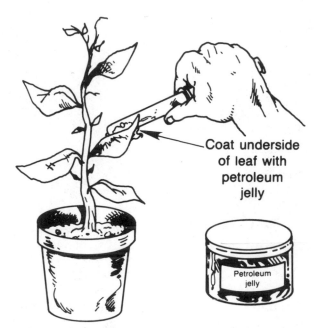

Coat underside
of leaf with
petroleum
jelly

Petroleum
jelly

Fig. 3-6. Coat the underside of the leaf with petroleum jelly to prevent air from reaching the stomata.

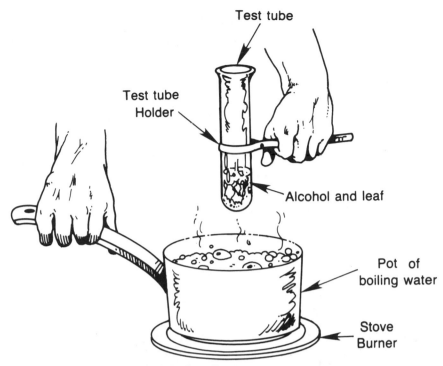

Test tube

Test tube
Holder

Alcohol and leaf

Pot of
boiling water

Stove
Burner

Fig. 3-7. Use tongs for added safety.

Going Further

1. Can a plant go without carbon dioxide longer if it doesn't have water? A cactus can go without water for long periods of time.

2. Experiment with the stomata on pine needles. Will the results be the same as for plants with deciduous leaves?

PROJECT 6
Say Cheese

Overview

The photosynthetic process gets its power or energy from the sun. In order for plants to thrive, the sun must strike the leaves. This is why leaves are not stacked one on top of another. Instead, leaves spread out side by side, looking for openings where sunlight will shine through. This layer of leaves is called the "canopy layer" in trees.

In the forest, the canopy layer is very thick and little or no light comes through. Consequently, we will hypothesize that trees have leaves that maximize their contact with light.

Materials

- camera

- black and white film

- an area in a forest where you can photograph trees (The trees must be healthy and free from infestations or diseases that would affect the growth of leaves.)

Procedure

Pick an area in the forest where trees are growing and healthy and that do not seem to have much undergrowth or ground cover—the seedlings and saplings, shrubs and herbs that grow on the ground. Stand beneath the trees, point the camera up at the canopy layer and take several photos. Be sure not to point the camera at the sun.

Find several areas that have more ground cover. Areas where more light comes through the canopy should have more. Quantify the area by counting or photographing the ground cover then photographing the canopy layer.

It might help if you make several sets of photographs. Number the undergrowth photos and letter the canopy photos, being careful to match the right canopy photo with the right undergrowth photo. Write them down as you take them, if that will help.

Compare the canopy photos with the undergrowth photos to determine if the size of the canopy layer affects the amount of sunlight that comes through and, consequently, the amount of undergrowth. Was your hypothesis correct?

Note: This project could also be classified in a science fair under the environmental science category.

Going Further

1. Are there specific species of understory plants that are shade tolerant? Would you be able to identify where they can be found by merely looking at the canopy layers?

2. Can the understory's age be determined by observing the changing canopy layer (several seasons)?

PROJECT 7
Food for Plants: Carbon Dioxide
(Adult Supervision Required)

Overview

Plants require water, carbon dioxide, and minerals to thrive. From sunlight and chlorophyll they produce food, which is carbon dioxide. If plants are given more food, carbon dioxide, will they grow better?

Materials

- three-foot trough or tube with an opening at one end and containment area at the other end
- healthy plants (each with five or more leaves)
- small aquarium
- dry ice (frozen carbon dioxide) **Caution: dry ice can burn skin. Always use tongs**
- tongs
- several books or a box

Procedure

Set up the tube, plant, and aquarium as shown in Fig. 3-8 and place it in the sunlight. Place a control plant near the experiment, but do not let it receive extra carbon dioxide.

The plant should receive carbon dioxide that is neither heated or cooled, that is why the tube is used. The tube allows the carbon dioxide to evaporate, flow down the tube, and arrive in the area of the plant. Although the gas will warm some, it is not significant.

Because carbon dioxide is heavier than air it should flow down. That is why the books or box is used. (In the sunlight, the dry ice will warm, producing a gas (carbon dioxide).) The gas will flow through the tube to the aquarium, warming some.

Add the carbon dioxide (dry ice) regularly, about every other day. Always add the carbon dioxide in sunlight in the early afternoon. This allows photosynthesis to take place for several hours while the extra carbon dioxide is present.

Observe the test plant and the control plant after several feedings. Conclude whether your hypothesis was correct, based on the results.

Labels in figure: Hollow tube · Aquarium tank · Dry ice placed 4″ from end · Books or boxes to make a slight downward slope · Plant

Fig. 3-8. Dry ice is placed near the plant to test if carbon dioxide increases growth.

Going Further

Do the experiment on several outdoor plants. Construct a barrier with an outerframe, such as plant stakes with cellophane or rubber sheeting. Add carbon dioxide twice a day for five or six days.

4

Hydroponics

There are many good reasons for growing our own plants and vegetables. But some people dislike the backbreaking toil required to maintain an outdoor garden. The smell of fertilizer, biting bugs, and hot summer heat can put a damper on the joys of gardening. Plants can be grown more comfortably indoors using a technique called hydroponics. Hydroponics is a unique nutrient solution that can grow plants without soil.

Some plants are naturally hydroponic, dune grasses that grow on the beach, for example and seaweed which is used in Japan as food.

Many plants that have traditionally been grown in the ground (geoponics), can now be grown without soil by feeding them with a nutrient liquid. In 1930, Dr. William Gericke, a professor at the University of California, grew a 25-foot tomato plant using a nutrient solution. Dr. Gericke discovered the exact proportion of mineral nutrients that was required for growing tomato fruit. He is credited with coining the term "hydroponics."

Advantages of Hydroponics

The advantages of hydroponics over soil growing are many. Since the amount of land available for producing food is decreasing because population is increasing, growing plants in a soil-less culture is very important. Often, fruits and vegetables have improved freshness and higher nutritional value.

Hydroponically-grown plants can be grown inexpensively and more environmentally sound. There is little wasted water and solution since plants are container grown (water conservation). Since plants are given all the nutrients they need, root system are often less extensive. This means that minimum space is needed, and more plants can be grown hydroponically in a smaller area. Pesticides are unnecessary. Indoor growing minimizes pest control, especially for large pests such as rabbits. There is better control of temperature inside as well. Artificial light can be used. Crops can be grown all year round, without fear of frost.

A great advantage to indoor hydroponic growing is that it does not require backbreaking work. Anyone with a handicap that makes it difficult for them to work on the ground can set up a garden on a bench or table top. Finally, root rot, which occurs if soil remains too moist, can be better controlled.

The Need For Hydroponics

Because water and nutrients are conserved, growing food hydroponically is well suited to desert regions or other areas where water is scarce.

Hydroponics will be especially important in the space-age. Space stations, moon bases, and long-term vehicles will essentially be separate planets, and will need to grow their own food. Soil might not be available. Soil is too heavy to carry into space and whatever soil was initially taken would be all that was available.

Although sunlight-producing energy will be available, and hydrogen could be gathered in outer space, obtaining additional oxygen would be a problem. Therefore, all water, or waste products of water, will have to be re-used.

Checking Your Water

Water used to grow plants hydroponically must be checked for pH—potential hydrogen—acidity (sourness) or alkalinity (sweetness). The pH cannot be too low or too high, otherwise any nutrients in the solution are locked up and unavailable to the plant.

pH is measured on a scale from 1 to 14, with 7 being neutral, 1 being acid, and 14 being alkaline (see the graph in Fig. 4-1). There is a factor of 10 between each value on the scale. For example, a pH of 5 is 10 times more acidic than a pH of 6, and a pH of 4 is 100 times more acidic than pH 6.

A very desirable pH for hydroponics is between 5.5 and 6.5. The chart in Fig. 4-2 shows the best pH ranges for many popular vegetables.

Measuring pH can be easy and inexpensive with litmus paper (pH paper). Litmus paper and other test kits for checking the pH of water are available through many scientific supply houses, some of which are listed in the source list. Swimming pool test kits can be used, although they usually do not have a wide pH range and your water could read off the scale. If you need to change the pH of your water, Eco Enterprises and other

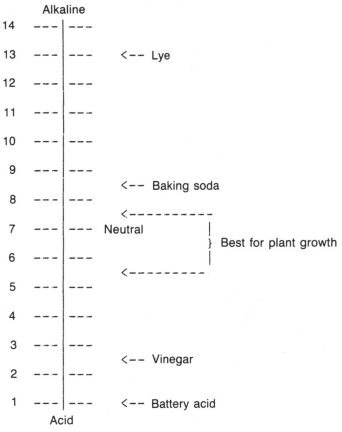

Fig. 4-1. The pH scale.

pH 5.0 - 5.6	pH 5.2 - 6.0	pH 5.6 - 6.8	pH 6.0 - 7.2
potato	eggplant	beans	beet
sweet potato	pepper	carrots	broccoli
watermelon	tomato	corn	cabbage
		parsley	cucumber
		parsnip	endive

pH 5.6 - 6.8	pH 6.0 - 7.2	pH 6.4 - 7.6
pumpkin	leaf lettuce	asparagus
salsify	muskmelon	cauliflower
swiss chard	peas	celery
turnip	radish	leek
	rhubard	head lettuce
		onion
		spinach

Fig. 4-2. The best pH watering range of common vegetables.

hydroponic supply firms listed in the source list sell chemicals you can add to your water to bring it into the range you need. Also, you can add potash to water if it is too acidic, or add sulfuric acid if it is too alkaline. Use extreme caution when dealing with sulfuric acid; it is highly caustic and can burn skin. Have an adult dilute some before using.

Chlorine is added to many municipal water supplies to kill bacteria and make the water more healthful to drink. Chlorine, however, in large quantities is not good for plants. In order to reduce the chlorine content, set tap water out for three days, as you would do for tropical fish. The chlorine will evaporate and the water will become room temperature. Usually, water right out of the tap is quite cool. Cold water can be a shock to plants.

Water conditioners used on home water supplies might remove minerals that are desirable to plants. Avoid using water that has been processed by a water conditioner. "Hard" or "soft" water should not make any appreciable difference to your plants. Hard water contains salts of magnesium and calcium, which is generally good for plants.

Watering plants in hydroponics is also feeding, and must be done on a regular schedule or plants become weak. A good rule of thumb is to match watering to how a plant uses nutrients. If there is a lot of sun, give it lots of solution. If there is little sun, give it a little solution.

The water in the growing container should not entirely cover the roots. Plants must be allowed to breath, and so most part of the root system (Fig. 4-3). In terrestrial plants, nitrogen fixing bacteria changes atmospheric or free nitrogen into a form that can be used by plants. In hydroponics, nitrogen fixing bacteria are eliminated. Therefore, nitrogen is a very important added ingredient.

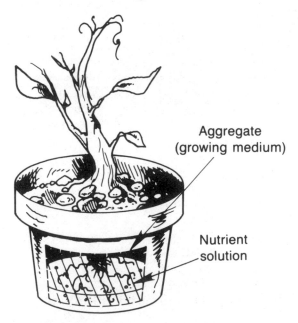

Aggregate
(growing medium)

Nutrient
solution

Fig. 4-3. Soil or a soil substitute should keep roots moist and aerated.

Normally, you will use water from your kitchen sink in your experiments. You might want to experiment with rain water, however. Rainwater is mostly pure, but particulate matter can be in it if you live near a big city or industry, which is undesirable.

Nutrient Solutions

Nutrient solutions are a mixture of water and mineral salt fertilizers. They provide all of the nutrition that a plant would naturally get from rain and soil. Before you begin hydroponic experiments you must make or purchase solutions.

There are hundreds of formulas, some for specific plants, some for growing larger vegetables or growing brighter flowers. Several standard nutrient solutions are the U.S. Department of Agriculture's formula, and a general purpose formula that has been well tested throughout the years. Ready made powders that can be mixed with water are available inexpensively from a list of suppliers, which are listed in the source list.

If you want to mix your own solution, use one of the formulas listed below.

United States Department of Agriculture formula:

0.5 grams of ammonium sulfate

3.3 grams of potassium nitrate

1.5 grams of monocalcium phosphate

2.2 grams of magnesium sulfate

2.5 grams of calcium sulfate

trace amount of iron sulfate

Mix with 1 gallon of water

General Purpose formula:

3.0 grams of sodium nitrate

1.0 grams of potassium sulfate

1.3 grams of superphosphate

1.0 grams of magnesium sulfate

trace amounts of trace elements

Mix with 1 gallon of water

It is possible to create a solution from items found around the home or local market. The "Poor Man's" solution consists of:

1 tablespoon	5-10-5 standard plant fertilizer
1 teaspoon	Epsom salts
1 teaspoon	washing ammonia

Mix with a gallon of water

The "Grocery Store Solution:"

1 teaspoon	baking soda
1 teaspoon	Epsom salts
1 tablespoon	saltpeter
1 tablespoon	washing ammonia

Mix with a gallon of water

In these formulas, Epsom salts provide magnesium sulphate, and saltpeter provides sodium nitrate. The chart in Fig. 4-4 shows most of the known elements used by plants and the function they perform.

If you choose to make your own solution using one of the first two formulas, we recommend purchasing chemicals that are agriculture grade rather than laboratory grade. These are less expensive and might contain small amounts of impurities, which is desirable.

Growing Mediums

When plants are grown in a 100 percent nutrient solution, it is sometimes referred to as "aquaponics." This technique requires some sort of support for the plant. Usually, it is easier to grow plants in some kind of growing "medium" or soil, which can help support the plant's root system. As long as the growing medium, sometimes referred to as an "aggregate," does not add any nutrients to the plant, the method is considered to be hydroponic. Some materials that can be used as "soil-less" growing mediums are: sand, gravel, LECA—light expanded clay aggregate (see the photo in Fig. 4-5), small stones, colored gravel, cinders, volcanic lava, charcoal, sawdust, vermiculite, and perlite.

Vermiculite is a natural occurring mineral containing millions of tiny cells. These cells store air and water. It does decompose over time, but does not affect soil pH and has no food value for plants. Perlite is light porous pebbles. Both vermiculite and perlite can be purchased at garden and hardware stores.

Each medium has its advantages and disadvantages. Its purpose is to allow moisture and oxygen to get to the plant's roots and to physically support the plant. In nature, earthworms crawl through the ground to aerate the soil. You can use most any inert object as a growing medium.

ELEMENTS	SOURCE AND FUNCTIONS
Carbon	Gets carbon from CO_2 in the air through leaf stomata. Carbon, oxygen, & hydrogen manufacture carbohydrates (food for the plant).
Oxygen	Gets through stomata (atmosphere) and through roots (water).
Nitrogen	Required in production of leaves and stem growth—stimulates green growth. Source: Potassium nitrate, sodium nitrate, and calcium nitrate {which also provides potassium, sodium (not needed by plants), and calcium, water (H_2O)}.
Phosphorus	Develops flower blooms and fruit, and good roots. Source: Ammonium phosphate (best source).
Potassium	Gives good strength and turger (woody stems), and pulp of fruit. Source: potassium sulfate. Common source: potash and saltpeter. (saltpeter is potassium nitrate).
Calcium	Root growth. Aids in absorption of potassium. Gives structural rigidity. Source: calcium sulphate.
Magnesium	Distributes phosphorus throughout plant. Aids in chlorophyll production. Source: magnesium sulphate, magnesium nitrate. Common source: Epsom salts (mag. sulphate).
Sulphur	Used in energy production (protein formation).
Iron	Used in chlorophyll production. Source: ferrous sulphate, feric chloride.
Manganese	Assists absorption of nitrogen. Source: manganese sulphate, manganese chloride.
Zinc	Used in energy transference process.
Boron	Makes cell walls permeable to sugars. Source: boric acid, trace amounts found in copper sulphate and zinc sulphate. Common source: Borax.
Copper	Used in chlorophyll production.
Iodine	Intensifies leaves' green color.
Chlorine	Controls water intake and transpiration.
Molybdenum	Used in the process of assimilation.
Cobalt	Aids in formation of vitamin B-12 and DNA synthesis.

Fig. 4-4. Table of plant elements and their importance.

Fig. 4-5. LECA, or light expanded clay aggregate, is commonly used in hydroponics.

Lettuce has been grown on a sheet of styrofoam, although this is not the best medium. Sometimes the best mediums are combinations. A mixture of equal parts vermiculite, perlite, and peat moss is often used. Even soil in which all the nutrients have been used up can be used for your experiments.

Experiments in hydroponics can grow plants in 100 percent solution or in a soil-like material that has no nutrient or food value for the plant.

Considerations

As you prepare for your experiments, keep in mind that nutrient solutions must be changed frequently. This is to renew oxygen and minerals. Furthermore, as water evaporates, the solution can become more acidic.

The solution should not be in direct sunlight or algae can grow. If you are using a test tube to grow a clipping, or growing a seedling in a jar, cover the area where the solution would be exposed to light. If, during your experiments, you find large quantities of green algae in the container or on the roots, remove the plant. Rinse it thoroughly under running tap water. Completely clean the container or use a new container. Place the plant back into the container and add new nutrient solution. Algae growth is unattractive, smelly, and competes with the plant for nutrients.

It is important to keep a close watch on your plants for any signs of trouble. If trouble occurs, try to find out what is going wrong and make corrections quickly. When a child cries, he is trying to tell you something. You must determine the cause. Is he wet, tired, hungry? With plants, the leaves are your guide. The chart in Fig. 4-6 shows some common symptoms and causes that can occur.

Symptom	Causes
Yellow or pale leaves	Nitrogen deficiency Magnesium deficiency Sulfur deficiency
Purplish or reddish leaves	Phosphorus deficiency
Small leaves	Boron deficiency
Thin foliage	Zinc deficiency
Green veins on yellow leaves	Iron deficiency
White areas around veins in leaves	Oxygen deficiency
Wilting	Hydrogen deficiency
Poor growth	Nitrogen deficiency Water pH out of plant's range Insufficient aeration of roots Calcium deficiency Sulfur deficiency Manganese deficiency Chlorine deficiency
Poor resistance to diseases	Potassium deficiency
Small, thin skinned fruit	Potassium deficiency
Weak stalks	Potassium deficiency

Fig. 4-6. Symptoms and causes of common plant problems.

Plants might loose some leaves when they are transplanted or moved from one location to another. This does not necessarily mean there is a problem. It is a normal adjustment while the plant gets acclimated. Keep watching for new shoots and leaves. Remove yellow leaves. Trim brown tips. This can be done with scissors and does not harm the plant.

The biggest problem in hydroponics is keeping the water level at an optimum level. If you do not tend to your plants for a few days, water can evaporate, exposing too much of the root and dehydrating the plant.

Hydroponics can be done outside, but you must shield plants from strong winds and too much rainfall. Also, there are more temperature extremes outside, as well as an increased risk to diseases and pests.

When mixing hydroponic solutions, do not get carried away and put too much fertilizer in the water. If there are too many nutrients in the water, the plant actually looses water to the solution and dehydrates.

Keep plants away from hot stoves, fumes, gas ranges, and cigarette smoke. Occasionally, spray a mist of water on all leaves to remove dust and particles that could clog the stomata.

While the best sunlight might come from a window, watch your plant to see if it dislikes the winter cold near a window at night.

Learn about the type of plant you are growing. Problems can arise because you are not growing the plant in the environment that it likes, making you think your experiment is a failure. Some plants, such as lettuce, like cool temperatures. African violets, forget-me-nots, impatiens, and wax begonias like a lot of shade. Peas prefer full sun. If you are growing ornamental plants near a window, rotate them to maintain an even shape.

In hydroponics, you must be alert to the differences in plant species. Some plants adapt better to growing hydroponically. A good example is lettuce. Lettuce is hydroponically-grown indoors in a very large production situation. One operation in the southern United States grows more than 5 million heads of lettuce a year hydroponically.

Generally, easiest plants to grow are, lettuce, dwarf tomatoes, strawberries, and cucumbers.

Containers

Beginning a hydroponic garden requires innovative thinking. A germination bed must not hinder the seed growth. The root system must grow down and the stems must grow up. Some seeds cannot have pressure on their sides, or they will not germinate. They must be free to push open their shells.

A variety of growing containers can be used, test tubes, wide mouth jars, or aquariums. An old sink, glazed earthenware, metal buckets painted with asphalt, and troughs can be used. Think about how the plant is to be supported. Dr. Gericke's technique used large, waterproof basins with wire grids to support the plant. The roots dangled down into the solution. A bedding of dried hay or peat moss covered the top to keep light out, moisture in, and let air freely circulate. When choosing a growing container, keep in mind that it must not rust; be affected by acid or alkaline; emit toxic substances; and it must be waterproof.

Are You Ready? Let's Grow!

Want to learn a new word or two? A hydroponic growing unit is called a "hydroponicum." If you grow plants hydroponically, you are called a "hydroponicist." Doesn't that title make you feel important?

PROJECT 1
Soiled But Not Dirty

Overview

Growing mediums provide nutrients, physical support, hold moisture, aerate roots, and offer protection for plants from predators. Different soils are better suited to particular species of plants. This experiment demonstrates how one species of plant will not adapt to four test soils as well as it does to the control medium. The control medium is the material in which the plant is naturally growing or is potted in when you purchase the plant. A hypothesis for this experiment might be that the test plants in four types of soil will grow better than the control plant in a certain order. For example, the plant species you have selected might not grow as well in sand and vermiculite as the control plant does, yet the plants in potting soil and soil from the backyard might grow better than the control.

Materials

- sand
- potting soil
- 4 containers
- soil from the neighborhood
- vermiculite (available in hardware stores and garden nurseries)
- 5 healthy plants (each with five or more leaves)

Procedure

Purchase five equally healthy plants. Gently remove one of the plants from the pot it came in. Rinse the root system to remove all existing medium. Replant it using one of the four test mediums, either sand, potting soil, soil from the neighborhood, or vermiculite. Use the same procedure for four plants (see Fig. 4-7). You must also remove the control plant from its pot. Rinse and replant it in the medium it came in. If the control plant is not replanted, it would not be a good control. Because each of the test plants have been rinsed (roots watered thoroughly) and their mediums loosened, the control plant must receive identical treatment.

A watering schedule must be maintained and the entire group of plants should receive the same amount of sunlight, air flow, temperature, and any other conditions. Monitor the plants over several weeks, or longer, and record your observations.

Conclude whether your hypothesis was correct based on the results of your experiment.

Use a fifth plant as a control plant. The control plant would not be replanted in another medium, but would remain in the soil it was purchased in.

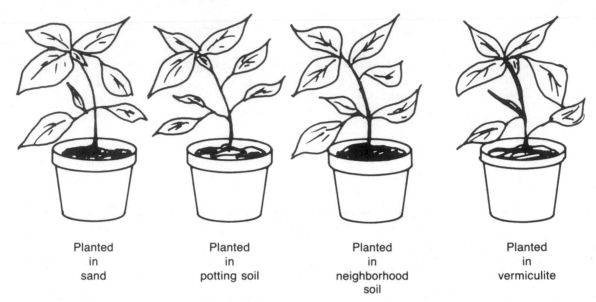

| Planted in sand | Planted in potting soil | Planted in neighborhood soil | Planted in vermiculite |

Fig. 4-7. Experimenting with different growing mediums.

Going Further

1. The species of plant selected for the above experiment would determine which medium would be best suited for its optimum health. Some plants require better draining soil, others require more support than sand or vermiculite offer. Experiment with different plants to determine the best for each type of medium.

2. Determine which plants are best suited to your environment—your backyard, flower box, indoor pots, or garden?

3. What, if anything, can be added to your existing medium to enhance its ability to grow additional plants?

4. Use a plant that flowers or bears fruit in the experiment. Evaluate the blooms or fruit and use this as a gauge of how well the plant is doing in its growing medium. Will the different mediums affect the different growth stages?

5. Do Bonsai (dwarf plants) require more exacting requirements for medium?

PROJECT 2
Soil Compactor

Overview

There are places in the woods and along fields where people have walked for many years. The soil is packed down (see the photo in Fig. 4-8). When soil is packed down it is hard for water to penetrate the soil. That is why there is less growth in an outdoor garden if the soil is not loosened. Pitchforks and other garden tools are used to turn the ground over and break it into small clumps. When there is no plant growth in compacted soil, runoff of rain water can cause erosion. Even in compacted soils and trails, weeds (unwanted plants) or grasses can grow. Some weeds and grasses are well suited to compacted soils.

Potted plants might suffer from compaction. This experiment tests whether compacted soils reduces health and growth in potted house plants.

Materials

- 3 house plants of the same species (at least one of which has compacted soil as its growing medium)
- fork or anything that can loosen soil from around the plant
- container

Procedure

Set up the compacted plant undisturbed as a control. Label this plant as the compacted soil plant. Take another similar plant and remove the soil from around the roots. Break up the soil completely in a separate container. Be sure to break up as many parts as you can that may be surrounding the roots. Replace the plant and the soil in the container. Label this plant as the completely loosened soil plant. On the third plant, break the soil up into large pieces, not just one big clump, but not as broken down as the soil in the completely loosened plant. Identify this as the partially loosened soil plant. Water all plants equally and keep all other factors (such as the amount of sunlight, wind disturbance, and temperature) the same.

Observe whether the loosened soil plant is healthiest. Make a chart similar to the one shown in Fig. 4-9. Observe for at least a few weeks. Define what you mean by the healthiest greener leaves, less brown leaves on the plant, new growth, more flowering, and other elements.

Conclude whether your hypothesis was correct based on the results of your experiment.

Fig. 4-8. Soil becomes packed down and contains less air where there is heavy foot traffic.

Going Further

1. Transplant natural plants to unused pathways where the soil is compacted and observe.

2. Study the natural "take-over" of plants in trails that are no longer used. Use photographs to compare or to indicate which species are pioneer plants that take over in compacted soil situations.

3. Measure the runoff of rainwater of compacted slopes as opposed to noncompacted slopes. A good way to do this is to go to the top of a slope and measure a distance of several feet from the top. In another area where the soil is not compacted, go an equal distance from the top and measure.

4. How long do potted plants take to become compacted? Should the soil be loosened frequently?

Date	Plant #1 loosened soil	Plant #2 semi-loose soil	Plant #3 compacted soil
Day 1			
Day 2			
Day 3			
Day 4			
Day 5			

Fig. 4-9. Sample log for recording *Soil Compactor* data.

PROJECT 3
Soil Has What It Takes

Overview

All of the plant life that is growing in the forest, whether it is a large tree or the smallest plant making up the ground cover, is grown in soil with water moving through it. The plant receives all of its nourishment from the moving water. This goes on from day to day, season to season, year to year. No one fertilizes this material. No one helps these plants. Yet, they still grow strong and healthy, apart from the intervention of man. What is it that they receive? Do they receive all the nutrient that they need? Hypothesize that all the nutrients plants need are available from the soil it grows in.

Materials

- 4 healthy house plants (each with five or more leaves)
- cheesecloth, about 1 yard long and 1 yard wide
- 12-quart bucket or container
- small pouring jar
- shovel
- twine
- measuring cup

Procedure

Obtain several healthy house plants. Using a shovel, scrape away the loose litter in a wooded area. Dig down and remove several shovels full of soil. Put the soil in the cheesecloth. Suspend the cheesecloth above the bucket either by tying it or having a helper hold it in place while you pour about 2,000 milliliters of tap water into the soil. After several minutes when most of the water has drained through, remove the dampened soil and cloth. Pour the water into another container. Place the soil back over the bucket and pour the same water through the soil again (see Fig. 4-10). Do this procedure five times. The liquid that you will then have is called leachate. This liquid will be used to feed half of the test plants. The other half will be the control group that receives only tap water.

Hypothesize that the plants receiving the leachate will grow better because of the nutrients leached out of the soil. Set up an observation chart. Water the plants with 200 milliliters every three or four days. All other conditions, such as temperature, amount of sunlight, etc., should be the same.

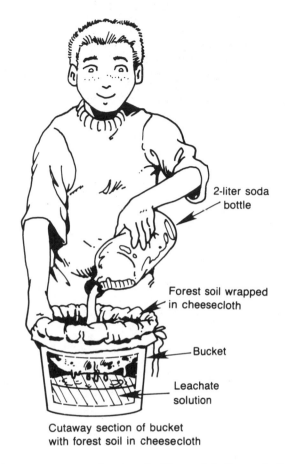

2-liter soda bottle

Forest soil wrapped in cheesecloth

Bucket

Leachate solution

Cutaway section of bucket with forest soil in cheesecloth

Fig. 4-10. Attempt to create a solution rich in nutrients for plants by leaching water through rich soil.

Test for at least several weeks. Conclude whether your hypothesis was correct based on the results.

Going Further

1. Set up a similar experiment using leached water taken from the soil surface up to 2 inches deep, another batch leached from 2 inches to 4 inches, and a third from 4 inches to 6 inches. Determine by growth which leachate is best for the plants.

2. Using water test kits, which can be purchased from scientific supply houses, test the leachate for the presence of various nutrients, nitrate, phosphate, and others.

3. Do chemical analysis of the different leachates comparing different layers.

4. Leach soil layers from different areas in your community where different types of plants are found.

5. Check the pH in leachates. Hypothesize that one soil increases the pH from what is measured in your tap water.

PROJECT 4
Kitchen Compost

Overview

Composting is the decomposing of refuse, the materials from various plants that are not eaten. This unwanted food can be put in a hole in the ground, leaves added, and lime mixed in, to help break down the material. Leaving the compost pile for long periods of time creates a rich, nutrient soil. This technique has been done since the days of old. The American Indians supposedly planted fish with their corn seeds. The fish would break down and provide additional nutrients for the plants.

Many materials are thrown away or discarded in our modern age, which could be composted. Composting requires some attention. It develops heat and must be covered with soil to keep from attracting insect and rodent pests. In this experiment, we will compose refuse from the kitchen and test its effect on house plants.

Materials

- month's supply of kitchen refuse, such as potato & onion skins, banana peels, carrot peelings, crusts of bread, unused and unwanted food—collect and process daily

- blender or food processor

- small area in the backyard

- several healthy house plants

- shovel

Note: The best time to start this experiment is early spring, when organisms in the soil can work on the compost.

Procedure

Dig a hole in the backyard about three feet deep and one or two feet wide. Save the soil you remove from the hole to make a layer of dirt to act as a cover after you pour in some material from your blender. Be careful that no one will accidentally fall into your hole. It might be a good idea to put up a fence to call attention to the hole and keep animals out.

After each meal, gather waste for the preparation. You might want to keep a small plastic trash bag by the kitchen sink to dump meal scraps into (see Fig. 4-11). Any organic material, such as fruits or vegetables that will decompose readily, can be put in a blender. Add only enough water to break the material down. The purpose is to crumble the food into very small particles.

Fig. 4-11. Keep a small plastic bag by the kitchen sink to collect food scraps for the compost pile.

Each night after the accumulated refuse has been broken down into very small particles, put it in the hole in the ground. Continue adding refuse for a month. Then, close it by spreading a cover layer of soil on top and waiting two months. During that time, you will have to turn the material over several times during each month.

After two months, remove it and mix it with the existing soil (one-to-one ratio) to use as a soil for the house plants that you have gathered. Remove the plants from their potting soil, wash their root systems off, and replace them in the pots with your new rich composted soil. Maintain the existing house plants as control plant.

Hypothesize that your composted soil will help the plants grow better. Make an observation chart. After four or five weeks, conclude which plants grew better.

Going Further

1. Set up many compost piles or holes of different materials. One hole could hold the waste from plates with food that people eat. Another could hold the scraps from peelings of only vegetables. A third could hold only scraps from fruits.

2. Set up three compost holes. Water one hole infrequently, the second more frequently, and the third hole more frequently to determine whether water will aid the decomposing process.

3. Add lime (use caution) to one hole but not to another. Lime helps the material break down the organic material. Lime can be purchased in hardware or gardening stores. Test the resulting soil by growing house plants in it.

PROJECT 5
Pass the Salt

Overview

There are large infertile areas on the earth's surface that could be made suitable for plant growth. Sandy soils such as that found in deserts could possibly be irrigated with seawater. Drainage is quick through sand. Certain cereals, flours, and other plants, might grow using saltwater with fast drainage. Saltwater contains very tiny microscopic decaying materials, which have a nutrient value that could perhaps be used to grow plants.

Materials

- 3 cereal plant seedlings (wild rice)
- 3 containers
- seawater (can be made or purchased)
- tap water
- three pans or saucers
- sand
- tape

Procedure

Fill three containers with sand. Put holes in the bottom for drainage. Have an adult help you bore the holes. Plant one seedling of each species in each container. Indicate which seedlings are in which containers on a piece of tape. Use only tap water for one group, a solution of half tap water and half seawater for the second group, and seawater only for the third group.

Control temperature, light, and other factors affecting plant growth. The only variable will be the watering with different solutions. Water the plants twice a day. Allow the solution to run out of the bottom and do not reuse the solution. Use about 200 milliliters of solution for each watering. Log observations in a chart as the one shown in Fig. 4-12.

Conclude whether your hypothesis was correct based on the results of your experiment.

Going Further

1. Determine if there is an optimum species for use with seawater.

2. Determine if there is an optimum solution using a mixture containing seawater.

3. What food-producing plants could be grown with massive setups to irrigate barren, sandy areas.

Date	Container #1 Tap water			Container #2 Sea water			Container #3 50/50 mixture		
	#1 Species	#2 Species	#3 Species	#1 Species	#2 Species	#3 Species	#1 Species	#2 Species	#3 Species

Fig. 4-12. Sample log for recording *Pass the Salt* data.

PROJECT 6
Who Are You Rooting For?

Overview

Hydroponics is growing plants in a liquid nutrient solution. Hydroponics plants receive all of their necessary nutrients through their root system, as do terrestrial plants grown in soil, which is called geoponics. Terrestrial plants send out long roots to gather more nutrients from the moisture in the soil. Do hydroponic plants require less root systems than terrestrial plants?

Materials

- 6 healthy plants in pots with soil
- hydroponic nutrient solution
- dark construction paper and tape
- 3 containers
- a support structure to hold plants upright when they are in a soilless environment

Procedure

Measure all six plants to be sure they are fairly equal. Set up a chart like the one shown in Fig. 4-13 for your measurements. Separate the plants into two equal groups. Remove three plants from their containers. Rinse the roots free of soil. Measure the root system (photographs would be helpful). Put the plants in containers with nutrient solution. Cover the outside of the container with a piece of dark construction paper to keep light from reaching the solution. Light encourages the growth of unwanted green algae in the solution. Remove three terrestrial plants. Rinse and measure their root systems. Replant them into the original containers using the soil that they came in.

On a regular basis, add water to each of the six plants. All other factors must be controlled. They must all get the same amount of light, temperature, and disturbance. The hydroponic plants might have to have a supporting structure to hold them up. Old milk cartons and any lattice work, twine, or angle iron works well, but keep in mind that the material must be strong enough to support the plant. You would not want to use twine to support a tomato plant, which can grow quite large.

After one week, observe the stems and leaves and record your findings. Continue to observe and record on a regular basis. After three weeks, evaluate the root systems in the terrestrial plants. Compare them in size to the root system in the hydroponic plants.

Measurements	Hydroponic Plants			Soil Plants		
	Plant #1	Plant #2	Plant #3	Plant #1	Plant #2	Plant #3
Starting Measurements						
Ending Measurements						
Comparisons						

Fig. 4-13. Sample log for recording *Who are You Rooting For?* data.

Conclude whether your hypothesis was correct based on the results of your experiments.

Going Further

1. Do a similar experiment using seedlings that you have germinated. Evaluate several different species of plants.

2. Start a similar experiment. Remove all plant materials from their containers. Cut more than half of the root system away. Place three plants back in soil and three in hydroponic environments. Be sure to water both sets of plants the same.

PROJECT 7
Time Will Tell

Overview

Some house plants grow all year-round, so do some food producing plants. Most plants we are familiar with have cycles that are in harmony with seasons. Some plant seasons run longer than others, ending in late October or early November. But most plants we are familiar with have seasons. They grow, bear fruit or flowers, and die back. Is there a biological calendar for plants? Do all plants require a winter dormancy period? How about hydroponically-grown plants? Can food be produced all year long? Hypothesize that food can be produced all year long indoors.

Materials

- bush green bean seeds
- 1 hydroponic container
- non-nutrient soil-less medium (vermiculite, perlite, sand, gravel, light expanded clay aggregate (LECA), or any combination)
- support device to hold the plant stems stable
- hydroponic nutrient solution
- enough sunlight for the plant to grow in the winter months (you can use indoor plant lights available at garden supply stores)

Procedure

Germinate the bush bean seeds. As they get larger, plant them in the hydroponic container. When they have grown more mature, stabilize their stems with a supporting structure such as the one shown in Fig. 4-14. Keep good notes on how many seeds germinated, how they grow, and how many seedlings survive. Quantify the number of green beans per plant when they reach maturity. This experiment will run all winter, so it is a long-term project. Be aware that plants can get cold by being too close to a window, or too hot by being near a heating duct.

Going Further

1. In the spring when all the plants have matured, measure the output of the whole indoor green bean garden against an outdoor bean garden and compare the results. Conclude whether the indoor hydroponic garden requires more or less work, produced more or less beans, and continued to flourish or die.

Fig. 4-14. Use thin columns of wood, a plastic milk carton, and some string to support plants.

2. Will bush green bean plants continue to yield vegetables if the temperatures remain the same and the plant doesn't head into a biological dormancy. How many yields of beans will you get, and at what point will the plant die? This could be a two or three year experiment.

3. Other edible plants that can be grown indoors are herbs. Can you locate several herbs that would continue to flourish indoors hydroponically? Will they have dormancy periods or can they be made to produce all year? Be advised that herbs do not require as much sunlight as other vegetables, they are quite shade tolerant.

PROJECT 8
Bright Is Beautiful

Overview

Plants require a certain amount of light to photosynthesize and produce food. Will plants grown in hydroponic solutions require greater quantities of light than plants grown in soil?

Materials

- four healthy plants of the same species
- a light source that can be controlled (perhaps a light on a work bench where natural light does not shine)

Procedure

Put two of the plants in soil and two in hydroponic solutions. Set up an observation log. Place both groups of plants in the light (see Fig. 4-15). Put one of the hydroponic plants and one of the soil growing plants next to each other to form a group. Remove this group from the light after five hours, but leave the light on the other two plants (one terrestrial and one hydroponic) for another five hours. Do this each day for several weeks. Hypothesize that the increased exposure to light will produce a greater growth in the hydroponic comparison than in the terrestrial comparison.

Gather data for several weeks, recording all observations. Photographs would be helpful. Conclude whether your hypothesis was correct.

Going Further

1. Place the plants closer to the lights to determine if the increased light makes a difference in the experiment. Use fluorescent lighting to reduce the heat given off by the light bulbs.

2. Is incandescent light better than fluorescent light? Be aware that light bulbs produce heat.

3. Is there an advantage to leaving the light on 24 hours a day, or do plants require some night rest?

Date	5 Hours of Light		10 Hours of Light	
	Hydro plant	Soil plant	Hydro plant	Soil plant

Fig. 4-15. Sample log for recording *Bright is Beautiful* data.

PROJECT 9
Solution To Pollution

Overview

Oil spills seem to be a way of life. Most of the oil spills we hear about on the radio and television occur in the ocean. Oil floats on water. The old saying, "Oil and water don't mix" is basically true. Petroleum products are a big pollution problem in our environment. Scientists have discovered bacteria that digest oil and cause it to degrade in the environment. These bacteria can help when there are oil spills. How does an oil spill effect plant life? Obviously, if oil coats a plant and prevents it from getting water, the plant will die. But, just because oil is present does it prevent the plant from getting water?

Materials

- 3 hydroponically-grown plants (house plants, tomatoes, lettuce, or others)
- cooking oil
- light motor oil (30 or 40 SAE weight)
- measuring cup

Procedure

Use one hydroponic plant as a control, keep all conditions exactly the same as the experimental plants. Pour about a one-inch layer of cooking oil on one of the experimental plants and a one-inch layer of motor oil on the other one (see Fig. 4-16). Put the plants where they will get plenty of sunlight. Be sure they get enough nutrient solution.

Hypothesize that the oil on both plants will either kill the plant, make it less fit for consumption, or cause it to become weak. Record data daily on the condition of all the plants. At the end of a specific period of time, four weeks for example, determine whether your hypothesis was correct. You might want to specify the period of time in your hypothesis so it is either correct or incorrect for that length of time.

Going Further

1. Will the oil be taken up into the fruit of a tomato plant? Test by running the experiment with a hydroponically grown vegetable or fruit producing plant, such as a tomato.

2. Locate some healthy plants growing outdoors. Stake out the area

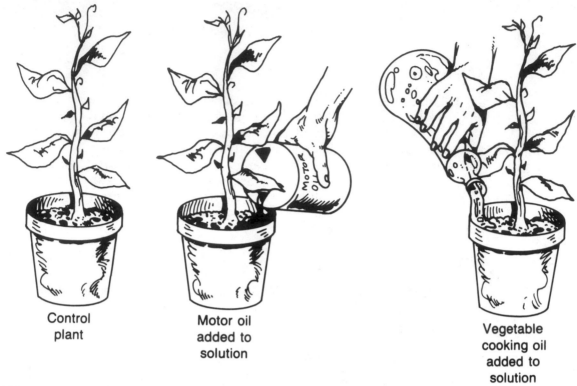

Control
plant

Motor oil
added to
solution

Vegetable
cooking oil
added to
solution

Fig. 4-16. Testing the effect of pollution on plants.

with small stakes and string. Pour one bottle of cooking oil over the area every week. Observe the condition of the terrestrial (soil grown) outdoor plants. Will the oil have an effect on their growth?

3. If the oil in the last experiment has an effect on plant growth, will the root system change because of the presence of the oil? Does it increase or decrease in mass? Will the plants attempt to find areas where water is oil free by growing runners or extended roots away from the oil?

PROJECT 10
Building Aggregates

Overview

Building aggregates are stone, brick, cinder block, and other materials used for building houses, roads, bridges, and other structures. These materials break down through weathering, rain, and various algae and mosses growing on them, which produce acids to break them down. The pH level of rain water, which is becoming more acidic as time passes, causes statues and buildings to wear away more quickly. Will building materials break down in solutions and release materials that are healthy to plants, or will they release materials that are unhealthy to plants? It is possible that they release no materials and cause no change in plants.

Materials

- red brick
- cinder block
- sea shells or crushed cement
- hammer
- burlap bag
- safety goggles
- 4 or 5 hydroponically-grown healthy plants

Procedure

Using a hammer, place the aggregate material in a burlap bag. Wear safety goggles and do not let anyone stand close without wearing goggles. Pieces of the material could fly when struck with a hammer. Be sure that the material is safely inside of the burlap bag. Do not pound on a surface that can be scratched or marked. Crush the material into a fine powder. Place it in the plant container with the normal hydroponic solution to feed the plant. Use one container-grown plant as the control and do not add any building aggregate. In each of the other containers, place crushed red brick in one, crushed sea shells in another, and continue with as many different types of crushed aggregate as you have.

Log and record your observations over a period of four or five weeks as shown in Fig. 4-17. Indicate whether one plant grows better than another. Be sure to change the solution containing the nutrients every week. At the end of the period, conclude whether aggregates placed in solutions helped, hurt, or had no effect on the plants.

Date	Red brick solution	Cinder block solution	Crushed cement solution

Fig. 4-17. Sample log for recording *Building Aggregates* data.

Going Further

1. Using a mildly acidic water (with a pH of around 5.5 or 6.0), place the aggregates you have crushed in the water. Measure if there is a change in the pH of the water. Using water test kits, measure for dissolved oxygen, nitrates, and potassium. Perform these tests immediately after one day and again after five days.

2. Determine whether trace elements have increased because of the aggregate.

3. Determine if the aggregates break down by mass. Determine mass before placing it in solutions. Then leave them in solutions of varying pH levels, evaporate the liquid to dry them out, then weigh them again. Use a very accurate balance beam scale. Conclude whether any material has entered the solution from the aggregates based on the mass comparisons.

5

Stimulation

The high-power lines such as the ones in Fig. 5-1 that crisscross our country have been subject to many complaints from people living near them. They believe that these power lines are to blame for some of their afflictions, or that they cause poor crop growth.

It is true that the flow of electric current in the line radiates an electromagnetic field. This causes an alignment of particles. Is their any truth to the tales that crop growth is affected by electric lines?

Plants respond to stimuli. Plants are mobile, but they move so slowly that we do not notice the motion of their leaves, stems, or roots. There are a few unusual plants that respond quickly to a stimulus, such as the mimosa tree, whose leaves fold when the surface of the leaves is touched, and the Venus-Flytrap whose jaw-like leaf arrangement closes shut when a fly lands inside it.

Plant stimulation includes motion, electrical, radiation, sound, gravity, chemical, water, light, and touching. If a stimulus causes a response in a plant, it is called a "tropism." This is a movement response, not a growth responds. The behavior will either be a movement toward or away from the stimulus. If someone pokes your arm with a sharp pencil, you will probably move your arm away. Similarly, if you place a plant in sunlight, its stems will turn in the direction of the sun.

Tropisms are categorized by their stimulus. As shown in Fig. 5-2, the categories include: geotropism, a response to gravity; phototropism, a response to light; chemotropism, a response to chemicals; thermotropism, a response to temperature; hydrotropism, a response to water, and thigmotropism, a response to touch. All of these responses occur naturally.

Fig. 5-1. Some people who live under power lines claim that the electricity flowing in the lines are to blame for poor crop growth and physical ailments.

Tropism Name	Plant Responds to Stimulus
Chemotropism	A response to chemicals
Geotropism	A response to gravity
Hydrotropism	A response to water
Phototropism	A response to light
Thermotropism	A response to heat
Thigmotropism	A response to touch

Fig. 5-2. Table of plant tropisms and definitions.

PROJECT 1
Watch The Birdie

Overview

Plants respond to sunlight, primarily because plants need sunlight to carry on photosynthesis to make food. This response is defined as phototropism, "photo" meaning light and "tropism" meaning movement. It is a response to an external stimuli. All plants strive for sunlight. They might climb tall trees to get sunlight or grow along the ground toward openings where sunlight is more abundant. The more sunlight, the greater they grow.

Materials

- several house plants (large rubber tree plant works well)
- sunlit window
- piece of paper
- masking tape

Procedure

Draw a circle on the piece of paper, marking it at each quarter point on the circle (90 degree intervals). Place the paper beneath the container that holds the plant. Use a small piece of masking tape on the table as a reference mark (see Fig. 5-3) as a guide so that when you turn the plant, you can determine how much of a circle the plant has turned—quarter, half, full, etc. . . .

After the plant has been in the sunlight for three or four days, you will notice that the leaves of the plant are facing the sunlight. Turn the plant approximately one-quarter of a circle, or 90 degrees. The entire container of the plant will turn, therefore the leaves will be facing perpendicular to the light coming in the window. Make a log and observe the direction the leaves are facing. Record their position in the morning and again in the late afternoon. Hypothesize that the plant will have its leaves facing the sun within a few days, depending on the presence of sunlight. Record your data on a daily basis and determine whether your hypothesis was correct.

Going Further

1. Once the plant is completely facing the sun, turn the plant one-half a rotation (180 degrees) and note whether all the leaves turn in the same direction to arrive back facing the sun. Do some of the leaves turn to the left and some turn to the right? Can you determine any

Masking tape

Fig. 5-3. Set up for the project *Watch the Birdie*.

significant reason why the leaves turn in the direction they do? Do some leaves turn to the left and some turn to the right in order to reach sunlight? After the leaves are completely facing the sun, rotate back 180 degrees in the opposite direction. Now which way do the leaves turn?

2. Plants have a tip that will usually determine the way the entire stem bends due to phototropism. Experiment by blocking and exposing light at the very tip of the stem. You can use aluminum foil as a blocking mechanism to cover parts of the stem. This is a hormonal response to light.

3. Construct a tall box, approximately two- and one-half to three feet tall. Place baffles in the box to allow the growing plant to grow around the baffle and toward the light as shown in Fig. 5-4. Construct the first baffle approximately one inch above the height of the plant. Place a hole in the box above the baffles, that will allow light to shine in. Determine whether the plant will grow around the baffle and toward the light. Then, above that baffle, construct another baffle that fills up two-thirds of the box. Its opening should be opposite the first baffle. Consequently, is it possible to train a plant to grow around baffles toward the top of the box?

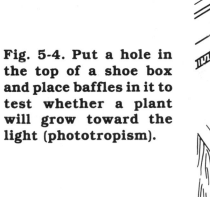

Fig. 5-4. Put a hole in the top of a shoe box and place baffles in it to test whether a plant will grow toward the light (phototropism).

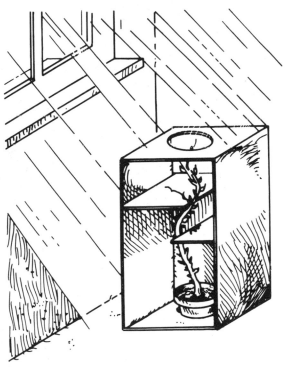

PROJECT 2
Nature's Herbicides
(Adult Supervision Required)

Overview

There are plants in nature that produce chemicals that restrict the growth of other plants, which is called chemotropism. An excellent example is the black walnut tree. There are many plants that cannot grow underneath the black walnut tree because the rain water washes over the leaves and goes into the ground, restricting the kind of plants that can grow there. In this experiment, we are going to see if the black walnut tree leachate has an adverse effect on certain weeds and grasses.

Materials

- bushel of leaves from a black walnut tree
- large pot
- section of lawn with grass (one square foot)
- section of lawn with dandelions (one square foot)
- stove
- tape measure

Procedure

Gather the black walnut leaves, twigs, pieces of root, and nuts. In a large pot, fill about two-thirds full with water, place as many leaves in the water as possible. Boil the mixture for 20 minutes at the lowest possible heat, stirring occasionally. Use adult supervision when working with the kitchen stove. Remove the leaves but keep the water. Put in another batch of leaves and boil them for 20 minutes. Remove them and cook a third batch of leaves.

When all of the leaves have been boiled, remove them and continue to boil the solution for another 10 minutes to evaporate more water, creating a concentrated solution. When the solution has cooled, use about one cup to water the grass area and the weed area of the lawn. Water the rest of the lawn with regular water. Set up a log like the one shown in Fig. 5-5 and make your observations. The watering procedure should require about one cup of water every three days. To better control this experiment, set it up indoors. Take two, one square foot areas of grass and two one square foot areas of dandelions and place them on trays. You will need two

Observation Log

Date	Control		Test	
	Grass Area	Weed area	Grass area	Weed area

Fig. 5-5. Sample log for recording *Nature's Herbicide* data.

squares of each so that one can be the control area, receiving regular tap water.

When all of the water is used, observe and record the results. Was your hypothesis correct? Did you hypothesize that the black walnut leachate solution would damage the grass but not the weeds, or the weeds but not the grass, or maybe both?

Going Further

1. Use the roots for a similar experiment. Hypothesize whether the root solution has a greater affect than the leaf solution?

2. Use the twigs and make another solution.

3. Use the nuts and make another solution.

4. Try the solution on several different species of plants.

5. Determine the chemicals in the solution that change the growth of plants.

PROJECT 3
Rooting for Our Team

Overview

Most of the nutrients that plants need come through the soil, and therefore, through the root system. If plants need more of a certain nutrient, they might respond by moving (growing) toward the chemicals they need.

Materials

- 1 gram potassium sulfate
- 1½ grams super phosphate
- 3 grams sodium nitrate
- 6 healthy plants (each with five or more leaves)
- 3 one-gallon milk jugs
- measuring cup
- labels or tape
- paper

Procedure

Remove the plants from their soil pots. Completely rinse all soil from the roots of the plants. Re-dig the potting soil in the pots, making sure it is evened out. Remove a section of soil in the form of a one-inch cylinder in diameter. Place the root of the plant back in the pot. Do this with each of the six plants. Label the plants #1 potassium, #2 control, #3 phosphorus, #4 control, #5 nitrogen, and #6 control.

Place one gram of potassium sulfate in one gallon of water. Mark one-half of the plant pot for potassium sulfate solution. Use paper to wrap around the pot so that it encompasses 180 degrees. This side of the pot will receive the potassium solution along the edge. The other side of the pot will receive an equal amount of water. Label the other two solution pots with their chemicals, one-half with the chemical. Every two days, place one ounce of water on the side opposite the chemical and one ounce of chemical solution on the side with the label. Put two ounces of water in each of the control plants. Place all plants in a proper environment for growth. Your solutions should last several months. Keep the stock solutions out of sunlight to minimize algae growth. Continue the cycle for one month. Observe throughout the experiment and record the data (see Fig. 5-6). Examine the color of leaves, turgor, new leaf growth, or flowers.

Plant #1 & #2: potassium test
Plant #3 & #4: phosphate test
Plant #5 & #6: nitrate test

Date	Test Plant #1	Control Plant #2	Test Plant #3	Control Plant #4	Test Plant #5	Control Plant #6

Fig. 5-6. Sample log for recording *Rooting for Our Team* data.

Remove the plants, one at a time, note the side of the plant as you remove it so that you know which side of the root faced the chemical. For each plant, observe whether the root grew toward the chemical, away from the chemical, or if it was indifferent to the chemical. Evaluate each of the six plants. Use notes, diagrams, and photographs to record your results. Conclude whether your hypothesis was correct.

Going Further

1. Use other plants and place all three chemicals in one-third sections of pots, maintaining other plants as controls.

2. Combine the remaining solutions to use on outdoor test plants.

PROJECT 4
Plant Clock

Overview

Most plants know the difference between up and down. The side of a hill has many plants and trees growing straight up in the air, regardless of the slope of the hill. Trees that have been blown down from storms can produce "suckers," new trees growing from the stems of their roots. These suckers seem to grow straight up in the air, although most roots stay in the soil below the surface. This is called geotropism. It is a growth response to gravity. Will upside down and sideways plants continue to grow? Will they continue to grow in the strange direction they are facing, or will they grow straight up, responding to gravity? Hypothesize whether plants can grow and adapt to a new and unusual position.

Materials

- 12 clean test tubes
- 12 six-inch squares of cheese cloth
- 3 or 4 dozen elastic bands
- 12 eight-inch long pieces of string
- 12 germinated seeds, of the same species
- one 14" × 12" pegboard
- one 1" × 3" × 12" piece of wood
- hammer
- hand drill
- masking tape
- saw
- several wood screws

Procedure

Lay 12 test tubes around a circle on the pegboard in the form of a clock so that one tube faces open where the 12 would be, another where the one would be, and so on. Secure them to the board using elastic bands to go through the holes in the pegboard and over the tubes. Place a square of cheese cloth in each test tube. Place the seedlings in the cheese cloth. (These are used to maintain moisture around the plants' roots.) Use a piece of string to go across the opening and fix the ends to the sides of the test tubes using masking tape.

The tubes should be in the form of a clock facing many different directions. Moisten each piece of cheese cloth. Use the string to keep the seedling and the cheese cloth from slipping out of the test tubes. Stand the test tube holder upright. Use pieces of the 1″ × 3″ wood to construct a stand. Cut the 12-inch piece of wood into two pieces, one four inches long and one eight inches long. Affix the four-inch piece to the end of the eight-inch piece perpendicularly (see the photo in Fig. 5-7). Using wood screws, fix the clock structure to the upright wood piece.

Place the plants so that they are facing the sunlight. Keep the cheese cloth moist. You might have to moisten them every day. Observe your plants twice a day, morning and night. Log your observations on a chart such as the one shown in Fig. 5-8. End your experiment after several weeks of growing time. Your results should show what directions the seedlings grew in. Conclude whether your hypothesis was right.

Going Further

1. Would vine plants adapt better to this experiment?

2. Would a test tube taped to a slow moving device, such as a fan, create an artificial gravity?

3. What would happen in a situation of weightlessness, would plants respond to other stimuli besides gravity?

4. Conduct the experiment again using germinating seeds rather than seedlings. Determine which direction they germinate, up or down. Observe the root and the stem for several weeks. Be sure to keep the seeds moist. It might help to darken the tubes with sleeves of dark construction paper.

Fig. 5-7. Testing the effect of gravity (geotropism) on roots and stems on germinating seeds.

Seed Position	Date AM	PM	Date AM	PM	Date AM	PM	Date AM	PM
1 o'clock								
2 o'clock								
3 o'clock								
4 o'clock								
5 o'clock								
6 o'clock								
7 o'clock								
8 o'clock								
9 o'clock								
10 o'clock								
11 o'clock								
12 o'clock								

Fig. 5-8. Sample log for recording *Plant Clock* data.

PROJECT 5
Steam Heat

Overview

There are areas in the world where geothermal heating occurs. Geothermal heating is heat produced by the earth. Some plants might enjoy this environment. Others might find it unacceptable. When a plant responds to heat, either to avoid it or to move toward it, it is called thermotropism. Hypothesize whether the roots of a plant will move toward a heat source if the room temperature is around 60 degrees Fahrenheit?

Materials

- electric heater elements, used to wrap pipes and keep them from freezing (available at hardware stores)
- flower box
- potting soil
- 4 healthy house plants (each with five or more leaves)
- ruler
- thermometer

Procedure

Put one inch of potting soil on the bottom of a flower box. Put part of the heating coil in this layer. Make a loop two-thirds up the box in length and back again, as shown in Fig. 5-9. The heater line should run along the side of the box. Fill the flower box with another two inches of potting soil. Run another loop two-thirds up the box and back again, keeping it along the outside wall of the box. Cover the last loop with the remaining soil. Plant the four plants in the center of the box, equal distances from each other and from the ends of the flower box. Note which end of the box has the heating coil in it. The plant that is farthest from the heating coil will be the control. Use a log to record your observations. Water the plants equally. Place them where they can receive sunlight but not where the room temperature is above 60 degrees. This is an excellent fall or winter project that can be conducted in a garage that is only partially heated. Artificial light can help control the heat of sunlight.

Make observations daily. After three weeks of growth, evaluate the root systems. Carefully remove the roots from the soil to determine if the roots responded to thermotropism. Did they respond by growing toward the heat or away from the heat, or did they show no specific response at all?

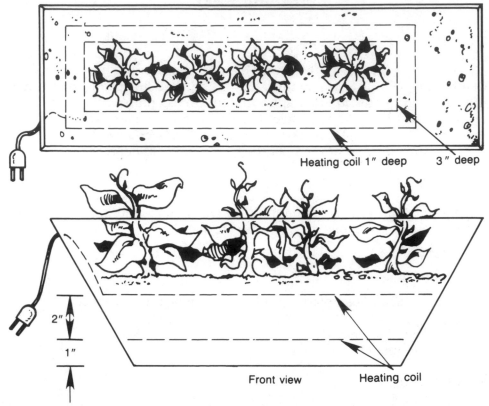

Fig. 5-9. Place an electric heater element under the soil as shown by the dotted lines.

Going Further

1. Support the pipe wrap electric heater element above the soil on small dowels (pencils or popsicle sticks) so that it is about three inches above the soil. Check the response of the plant to heat.

2. How do house plants respond to electric base board heating used in homes? Do they respond by moving toward it or away? What about hanging plants that are above a heater? Do they respond by growing toward or away from the heat?

3. Place a heating coil directly below the root growth. Trim the roots and replant the plant. Trim the roots of a control plant also and repot it. Does this help the regrowth of the root? This experiment can be quantified to determine the temperature of the soil below the heating element, above the element, at the surface, and in three places at the same levels, but without a heating coil.

PROJECT 6
Pet Plants

Overview

Plants can be stimulated by birds, beetles, snakes, butterflies, or other organisms moving through, or nesting on them. Does a plant grow better if it is stimulated by touch? Will it grow better in the presence of these natural stimuli?

Materials

- large terrariums or empty aquariums
- small stones
- topsoil
- lizard or other small animal that does not eat plants
- food and water for the animal
- screening
- 2 house plants

Procedure

Place a layer of stones at the bottom of both tanks for drainage. On top of that, place a layer of top soil. Transplant one plant into the tank where the animal will be living and the other into the empty tank. Set a container of water and food in the tank with the animal (see Fig. 5-10). Cover both tanks with screen to maintain the control equal. Water each plant. Be sure that the control plant receives the same conditions as the experimental plant. Place both tanks in sunlight.

Record data in a log for several weeks. Indicate whether the animal climbs on the plant (which is desirable), or if it spends any time on the plant. Note any changes in the plants growth—greater, less, or the same as the control plant. Conclude if your hypothesis is correct based on the results.

Going Further

1. House plants are often dusted. Will a dusted house plant which receives touch stimulation grow better than a plant that is not dusted? How can you control whether the dust is a factor or the touching is a factor?

2. Do plants that are in motion or that receive motion grow better than those that are immobile? Set an old record player on very low speed.

Fig. 5-10. Do plants grow better when they are frequently touched by other living organisms (thigmotropism)?

Place the plant in the center of the record player on a paper plate and let the record player spin for 5 or 10 minutes. Indicate the speed and length of time rotated. Use a control plant growing in the same area to compare to the plant in motion. Does motion increase, decrease, or have any effect on the plant? Maintain all other growth conditions.

PROJECT 7
Sound Off

Overview

Many people believe that plants that are spoken to grow better. They believe that if you spend a little time each day talking to your plants they will grow better. Could this be true, or are there other factors influencing the growth of the plants? Some studies suggest that all living materials have an aura around them, which is released by the life of the living organism. Is it this aura that affects the plants or the sound waves of the human voice? Hypothesize how the sound of a voice on a tape recorder will affect the plant as opposed to a natural normal speaking voice.

Materials

- healthy plants (each with five or more leaves)
- tape recorder with microphone and tape cassette

Overview

Speak into a tape recorder and record 20 minutes of normal speech. Place each of the three plants in separated areas that have equal exposure to the sun and equal temperature. Plant #1 will receive prerecorded sound only. Plant #2 will receive human voice sound from you. Plant #3 will receive neither. Place the plants some distance from each other, but in growing environments that have equal amounts of sunlight, temperature, humidity, and other factors. Set up a log for each of the three plants. Each day, turn on the tape recorder for plant #1 for 20 minutes and talk to plant #2 for 20 minutes. Read a story to it, perhaps a book you are reading for a homework assignment. Record the growth of the three plants. Water and care for all plants equally. At the end of three weeks, compare them and conclude if one grew differently than the others. Was your hypothesis correct?

Going Further

1. Do plants in music rooms grow better than plants not in music rooms?

2. Compare human voice with other sounds. Use a rock tumbler to create a noise.

Fig. 5-11. Investigating the effect of sound on a plant.

PROJECT 8
A Batch Of Plants

Overview

Normally, plants do not grow individually as they do in artificial situations, such as a home. Plants are usually surrounded by many other plants of different sizes and species. Do plants in the center of a batch of plants receive any value by being in the center? Are they less susceptible to insects and wind? Do they grow taller? It has been observed that trees in the middle of a batch of trees grow taller because they don't have to fight the wind. Also, the trees on the perimeter grew thicker; they required more strength.

Materials

- 1 dozen plants that grow tall, possibly zinnias
- measuring tape

Procedure

Batch the plants together. Transplant them or maintain them in their original pots. Place them in an open area and observe the interior plants to see if the ones in the center grow better. Maintain a log and make observations (see Fig. 5-12). Make specific observations on how the wind affects them when it is blowing. At the end of the experiment, observe the height and overall health of the plants.

Going Further

Study the trees in your area and select a large group of trees. Tie ribbons on them so that you can remember which trees you are studying. Observe whether the perimeter trees receive more wind or more light. The perimeter might also receive more pollutants from vehicles if they are located near a road. Make as many observations as you can. Draw a map of the area and the locations of the trees. Measure their girth and height. Conclude whether your hypothesis was correct.

Plant Number	Location (interior or exterior)	Number of Leaves	Height of Plant	Number of Leaves	Height of Plant
Plant #1					
Plant #2					
Plant #3					
Plant #4					
Plant #5					
Plant #6					
Plant #7					
Plant #8					
Plant #9					
Plant #10					
Plant #11					
Plant #12					

Initial Measurements Log:
Date: _____

Final Measurements:
Date: _____

Daily Observational Log

Date	Weather Observations	Plant Observations

Fig. 5-12. Sample log for recording *A Batch of Plants* data.

PROJECT 9
I Don't Feel Anything

Overview

Will plants respond without any stimulation? Stimulation deprivation is impossible to do. Although you could attempt to provide an environment with no sound or no movement, a plant must still have access to air for carbon dioxide and sunlight. We also cannot eliminate gravity. Hypothesize that a plant would respond by reduced growth to an absence, or at least a reduction, of stimuli.

Materials

- 2 healthy house plants (each with five or more leaves)
- box constructed with sound absorbing material such as rugs, scrap cloth, pillows, etc.
- sunlight

Procedure

Put one plant in the soundproof baffled box. Place the box away from the busy daily activities of humans in an area away from drafts but with sunlight. An attic window might be a good spot (Fig. 5-13) and a baffled box might not be needed. Place the plant on a firm nonmoving foundation. It should be isolated from any drafts. Allow sunlight, air, and infrequent watering to take place, watering only once every seven days or so. Be sure not to over water.

The control plant should be placed in an active household area where it is exposed to the busy activity of people. It should receive the same amount of sunlight and water as the experimental plant.

Run the experiment for three or four weeks. Gather data every five days. Quantify your data with measurements. Count the number of leaves. From your data, conclude whether your hypothesis was correct. Using more plants for both the test group and the control group would increase the validity of your results.

Fig. 5-13. Set up a plant in an area where it will receive the least amount of stimulation, such as near an attic window.

6
Transport

Transport is the movement of materials throughout the entire plant. Plants need water, minerals, carbon dioxide, and oxygen to survive. All of the cells must be fed, given water, receive oxygen, and must have waste removed. These processes are a continuous part of a plants growth, flowers, seeds, or fruits. Therefore, a system of transport must be available. In humans, the circulation system transports blood.

Some plants are "vascular," that is, they have vessels like miniature tubes of straws. These tubes transport large quantities of materials. If you live in a five-story apartment, you need stairs to get groceries and other items to the top floor and a way down to take the garbage out. Similarly, a plant must get water from the roots up to the leaves. Some types of plants, such as algae, mosses, and lichens have no tubes, and materials must come in contact with the outer cells. These are called nonvascular plants. Experiments with these simple plants are covered in Chapter 7. Whether a plant is vascular or nonvascular, materials must still be transported from cell to cell.

Movement of water in a plant is done through tubes called xylem. Projects dealing with the xylem involve transpiration (water leaving the plant) and respiration (water used by the plant). Food, in the form of sugars and starches, move through phloem tubes to be used by the plant cells or stored for future use. Movement of gases involve leaf and root structures. Other movement includes chlorophyll in the leaves, pollen in flowers, and movement from cell to cell by osmosis and capillary action.

In this chapter, we investigate the quantity of material, distances transported, and seasonal differences. Effects of pressure, temperature, and sunlight on plant transport is also tested and experimented with.

PROJECT 1
Sugar Tipped
(Adult Supervision Required)

Overview

All cells must be fed, given water, and receive oxygen to use for energy. The classic experiment for demonstrating transport is using colored water and a stalk of celery. We will expand on that experiment and see if celery will not only transport color, but also substances that we can taste, such as sugar and salt.

Hypothesize what you think will happen to celery stalks placed in water, water with food coloring, water with salt dissolved in it, and water with sugar mixed in.

Materials

- 4 clear glasses or glass containers
- food coloring (blue, red, yellow)
- tap water
- 1 geranium plant (optional)
- 4 stalks of celery of similar size and length
- 3 tablespoons of sugar
- 3 tablespoons of salt
- sharp knife
- hand lens
- masking tape or labels
- ruler

Procedure

Examine the stem from a herbaceous dicotyledon such as the geranium. Using a sharp knife, slice across the stem. Be very careful using a sharp knife, have an adult do the cutting. Look at the regularity in the circular bundle of hollow tubes inside the stem.

Examine a piece of celery, which is a monocotyledon. With a sharp knife, cut across the bottom of the stem of one stalk. Observe the outer covering with an interior of pith containing scattered hollow tubes.

Put about five or six ounces of water in each of the four glasses or containers. In container #1, add 10 drops of red food coloring. In container

#2, add nothing to the water. Add salt to container #3 and sugar to container #4. Use a crayon, masking tape, or stick-on labels, to label the contents of the containers. Stir each solution about 50 times.

Keep a record of your work. Indicate the time the celery stalks were placed in the solutions. Be sure to use stalks of similar size, age, and length.

Observe after three hours, six hours, and overnight. Keep notes on how you proceed and any and all observations made. After each observation, write down what has happened. Use a rule if the red food coloring moves up the stalk to measure the coloring's progress at each observation. The chart in Fig. 6-1 shows how you might record your observations.

After 24 hours, remove stalk #3 and #4. Taste a piece of each stalk with the piece cut from a section above the solution line in the glass. By tasting, determine if there is any salt and sugar. Without allowing others to see which sample they are tasting, have three or four family members or friends make choices if they can. Record their responses.

After gathering all of the data, study the results and determine whether or not your hypothesis was correct.

Going Further

1. Can other flavors such as vanilla and lemon juice be transported?

2. Will other colors travel faster or farther than red?

3. Does very hot or very cold water make any difference in how fast or how far the food coloring is transported?

4. Can living plants transport food coloring?

Time	Stalk in water	Stalk red dye water	Stalk sugar water	Stalk in salt water
1 Hour				
3 Hours				
6 Hours				
10 Hours				
24 Hours				

Fig. 6-1. Sample log for recording *Sugar Tipped* data.

PROJECT 2
Leave Me Alone

Overview

Plants take in water through their root systems and transport it throughout the entire plant for its own use. Some plants appear to release water at night. Do plants loose a measurable amount of water through their leaves?

Materials

- 3 hydroponically-grown plants (each with 10 to 12 leaves) that have been grown in a small, clear glass container, such as a test tube, vial, flask, or jar and be the identical size for all plants
- marking tape
- 3 four-inch squares of plastic food wrap
- black construction paper
- nutrient solution

Procedure

Label each of the three clear containers and number them 1, 2, and 3. Be sure to have the same amount of hydroponic nutrient solution in each container and mark the height of the solution in each. In container #1, remove all of the leaves on the plant. Wrap a piece of plastic food wrap around the stem, which will allow any water coming out of the stem to be collected. Remove half of the leaves from plant #2. Label the container and mark the height of the solution. Wrap a piece of plastic wrap around the plant to accumulate any water that might escape through the leaves. Leave all of the leaves on plant #3. Label the container and wrap the plastic around it. Surround all three containers with black construction paper to reduce algae growth caused by sunlight. Place the plants in sunlight.

Prepare a log indicating the moisture found in the plastic wrap each night. Remove the wrap and wipe it dry before the onset of night. Each morning, measure the quantity of water comparatively. Is there more moisture on plant number one, two, or three? Do the experiment for one week. At the end of the week, measure the level of solution in each container. As the solution in each container decreases, did more transpiration occur? Conclude whether your hypothesis was correct.

Going Further

1. Do tree leaves give moisture through the night to other organisms, such as insects or birds?

2. Does the change in temperature in the morning, which creates a dew on the grass, cause formation of moisture from the air, formation of moisture from the plant, or both?

3. Is moisture that leaves a plant pure? Could clean water be made from dirty water this way? By using large quantities of plants that transpire water each night from their leaves, can we create a freshwater system for our own consumption?

PROJECT 3
Big Leaf, Big Radish

Overview

Like other plants, radishes, carrots, potatoes, and beets get energy from the sun. They make food in their leaves, which are above ground, and send the food material below the ground, where it is stored. Does this mean that radishes that have more leaf surface will have bigger roots with stored food? Perhaps they just have bigger roots because they are left in the ground longer.

Materials

- 1 dozen healthy radish plants
- potting soil
- containers
- tape measure

Procedure

Plant the radishes in two rows in the containers. Provide nutrients, sunlight, and proper temperature. Allow the radishes to grow to maturity.

Remove pairs of radishes separated by 10 day intervals. Using a log such as the one shown in Fig. 6-2, measure the leaf surface of each leaf. Add the measurements together to get a total for each plant. Add the totals for two plants together and divide by two to get the average leaf surface of the plants.

Next, measure the edible portion of the radish—the root. Measure the circumference and measure the length. Multiply the circumference by the length. Add the two radish measurements together, divide by two to get the average, and record the result. Be sure to log all of your data.

After 10 days, remove two more radishes. Perform the same measurements and recordkeeping as on the original two plants. After another 10 days, do the procedure again. Run the operation a total of six times. Evaluate your data and conclude whether your hypothesis was correct.

Going Further

1. Do the experiment using carrots or beets.
2. Use a natural aquatic plant, such as a bullhead lily.
3. Use a wild carrot.

Date	Total Leaf Area	divided by 2 =	Average Leaf Area	Radish Length	times	Radish Circumference	equals Size	Average Radish Size/Set
1st Set Plant A	⎤ Added to			⎤ ×			= A ⎤ Add	⎤ divided by 2
1st Set Plant B	⎦			⎦ ×			= B ⎦	⎦
2nd Set Plant A	⎤ Added to			⎤ ×			= A ⎤ Add	⎤ divided by 2
2nd Set Plant B	⎦			⎦ ×			= B ⎦	⎦

Fig. 6-2. Sample log for recording *Big Leaf, Big Radish* data.

PROJECT 4
Food Or Flowers?

Overview

Is there a point in a plant's cycle when it does not continue to store energy? At some point, a plant might stop making food for storage and start making flowers, or seeds, to continue propagating. If this is the case, then the root would not store more food. The plant could then be harvested, because there would be no point in keeping the plant in the ground any longer.

Materials

- 6 food-producing, flowering plants (such as radishes)
- tape measure

Procedure

Maintain three sets of plants (two in each set), harvesting one set when the first bud of a flower begins to show. Log the date. Measure the size of the roots. Add your measurements together then divide by two to obtain an average. When the flowers blossom, remove the second set of plants. Measure the roots and record their sizes and the average of the two. Remove the third set of plants after the plants have produced their seeds and measure the roots of this set. Compare the size of the roots in each of the three harvests. Record your results in a chart such as the one shown in Fig. 6-3 and conclude whether your hypothesis was correct.

Going Further

Do the same experiment but substitute radishes for carrots, flowering plants, or a bullhead lily.

	Date	Root length	times	Root circum- ference	divided by 2	Root average
Set #1 plant A	Buds appear					
plant B						
Set #2 plant A	Flowers blossom					
plant B						
Set #3 plant A	Seeds pro- duced					
plant B						

Fig. 6-3. Sample log for recording *Food or Flowers?* data.

PROJECT 5
Red For Xylem
(Adult Supervision Required)

Overview

The tubes that transport water through a plant are called xylem. Can we identify the xylem in the cross section of a stem under a microscope? Is the xylem located throughout the cross section in a particular area, such as the outer circle, or is it interspersed throughout the stalk?

Materials

- 3 different plants
- microscope or very strong hand-held magnifying lens
- red food coloring
- small jar
- scissors

Procedure

Cut stems from several different plants. Observe the way the stem is organized. Is it organized by concentric rings or tubes in bundles or groups? Cut a second piece from the stem to observe under the microscope. Place the major stem portions in water with red food coloring mixed in it. The water will transport up the stem creating a red xylem. Observe the cuts that have no food coloring. Cut a cross section from each stem. Look at it with the magnifying glass or the microscope. Make a drawing of each stem. Try to identify the xylem in each of your drawings.

Cut a piece of the stem that transported the colored water up the stem. It might be best to wait overnight to allow the colored water to rise up the stems. Cut a cross section above the liquid level. Again, draw what you see, identifying the red tubes as the xylem. Match the drawings with your other drawings to see if you correctly found the xylem before the coloring process.

Going Further

1. Will a plant absorb the color with the water or allow only the water to pass through?

2. Identify different species of plants by how the xylem are organized in the stems. Divide them into monocots and dicots. Monocots have parallel veins and the xylem are scattered throughout. They usually have petals in groups of three, six, or nine, such as flowering plants. Dicots have branching veins and the xylem are arranged in rings and can be easily identified by their five petals.

3. Identify the xylem tubes in a cross section of a tree or branch cut. Note: The xylem is in the last growth rings.

PROJECT 6
Flowing Food
(Adult Supervision Required)

Overview

Trees, particularly sugar maples, produce a sap which humans use to make syrup. Birch trees also produce a sap. Hypothesize which trees will produce the greatest amount of sugar.

Materials

- hollow taping device to be driven into the tree
- container with a cover
- 2 test tubes
- test tube holder or glove
- Benedict's solution (can be purchased from a scientific supply house)
- iodine
- stove
- pot

Procedure

You will need permission to use a maple or birch tree in your area. Insert the tap into the tree and position the container to accumulate the sap that will drain out. After four or five days, collect the sap to evaluate for starch and sugar.

To demonstrate how to test for sugar in sap, put half a teaspoon of granulated sugar in a test tube, half filled with water. Using an eye dropper, put about 20 drops of Benedict's solution in the sugar water. Fill the small cooking pot half way full of water. Place it on a stove and bring it to a boil (CAUTION: an adult should be present when working around a stove). Shake the test tube and suspend it in the boiling water. Hold it in place by using a test tube holder, clothes pin, ring stand setup, or heat glove as shown in Fig. 6-4. When the solution heats up enough, you will observe a color change from the normal blue color of Benedict's solution. This color change indicates increasing sugar.

green → yellow → orange

This color change determines whether sugar is present.

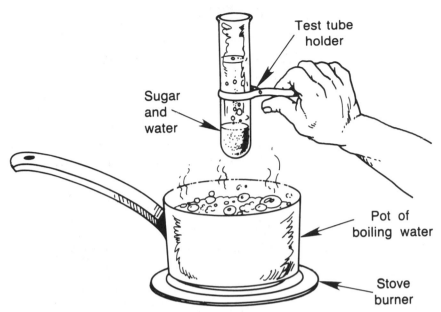

Fig. 6-4. Use tongs for added safety.

Now test for sugar in the sap as was done with the sugar above. Observe any color changes and record the results.

To test for starch, put iodine in the sap. A color change to blue or black indicates the presence of starch. Record your results.

Going Further

Measure the nutrients in different tree saps. Remove all of the moisture by evaporating the water. Measure the differences in quantity. Start with a gallon of each sap. How much syrup is produced by each?

PROJECT 7
Food But No Water
(Adult Supervision Required)

Overview

The phloem tubes pass food throughout the plant, just as the xylem are tubes for water. Can we accumulate materials above a girdling—a cut around a tree—if we cut only the phloem of a tree but not the xylem?

Materials

- hand saw
- permission to use a woody dicot tree (a perennial)
- iodine

Procedure

Girdle a portion of a tree, less than a quarter, so that you cut only the phloem and not the xylem. After two weeks, measure the quantity of starch above the cut. Although the water still flows up, nutrients that are ordinarily stored below the cut might be absent because the nutrients cannot flow past the cut through the phloem. Just above the girdling, the phloem should have an abundance of carbohydrates. Perform a test for starch. Remove several square inches of phloem material above the girdle cut. Mash the phloem and put several drops of iodine on it. Observe if there is a color change. It should turn blue or black, which indicates the presence of starch.

Going Further

1. Do the resins in a pine tree accumulate above the girdling area?
2. Is there an absence of starch below a girdle cut?

PROJECT 8
String Climber

Overview

Capillary action occurs in wicks and in small, diameter tubes. Would combining wicks and tubes produce a flow that was greater, faster, higher, or none of these. Form a hypothesis and run tests to prove it.

Materials

- twelve-inch capillary tubes (small, diameter clear tubing, available from scientific supply firms)
- thread
- string
- straws
- hollow, plastic coffee stirrers
- 2 clear glasses

Procedure

Fill two glasses with water to the same level (about one inch). Run a piece of thread through a coffee stirrer. Run a piece of string through a straw. Place the coffee stirrer and the coffee stirrer with string into one of the glasses (see Fig. 6-5). Observe capillary action. Does the stirrer with thread conduct water differently? Do the same procedure with a straw and a straw with string in it.

Going Further

At what size diameter does capillary action cease? Can you do this experiment with a garden hose and a piece of rope?

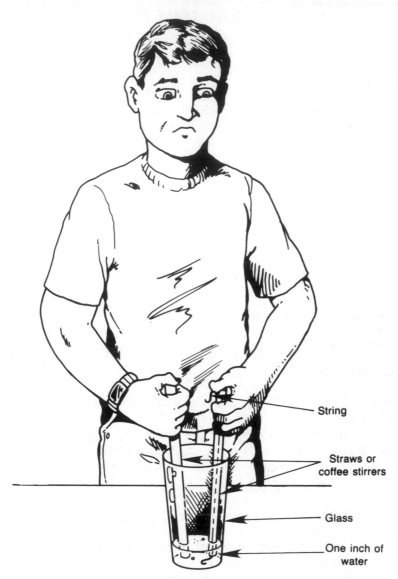

Fig. 6-5. If the opening is small enough, water can travel upward against gravity by capillary action.

String

Straws or coffee stirrers

Glass

One inch of water

7

Fungi and
Simple Plants

$\mathbf{S}$imple plants are plants that have very simple structures and functions and are nonvascular. Nonvascular plants have no vessels to transport food or water. In this book, we will consider ferns to be simple plants even though they are vascular because of their simple form, growth, and reproduction.

Nonvascular plants require water and food just as xylem or phloem plants, but have cells that transport materials through several layers of cells instead of tubes. Therefore, they must be low to the ground and in contact with moisture. Nonvascular plants have no true stems, roots, or leaves.

Fungi are organisms that do not photosynthesize. Instead, they receive nourishment from a host. A host is a living or dead plant or animal that provides nutrients, and sometimes lodging, to parasites and other organisms.

Lichens arc combinations of fungi and algae. Each of these two groups are considered scparately, except in the case of lichens.

Mosses comprise a large group of plants responsible for ground cover.

Bacteria, viruses, and protozoans are not considered in this book. They are best placed in the category of microbiology in science fairs.

Fungi have no chlorophyll and cannot produce their own food. They must receive their nourishment from dead or living organisms. Fungi that receive nourishment from dead organisms, are called saprophytes, and fungi that receive nourishment from living organisms are called parasites. Parasites are decomposers that return valuable material to the environment. Usually, the only part of fungi that is visible is its reproductive structure. The branching, main body of a fungus is usually deep inside its host.

PROJECT 1
Bad Bread

Overview

Bread molds form best on breads with no preservatives such as natural breads, which have little or no preservatives. Mold inhibitors are placed in mass-produced bread because they prevent, or at least reduce, the growth of mold. Spores, reproduction organisms found in fungi and molds, are responsible for allergies in some people. Therefore, be careful when handling and breathing around spores.

Will bread mold grow on other kinds of materials, or will it only grow on bread and products similar to bread?

Materials

- slice of carrot
- 1 orange
- small piece of uncooked beef
- cereal
- toast
- cake
- baby food jars (enough to match the number of materials you use)
- moldy piece of bread
- cotton swabs
- small shoe box
- measuring cup

Procedure

Put approximately one ounce of water in each baby food jar. Place a food sample in each jar. Remove some spores from a piece of moldy bread by moving a cotton swab across the top of the bread. Then wipe the cotton swab on a food sample such as the cake or carrot, on the jar. Discard the swab.

Using a clean swab, wipe the moldy bread again in a different area and place the spores (inoculate) on another food sample. Repeat this procedure for all of your food samples. Be sure to use a clean swab for each sample and an untouched area of mold.

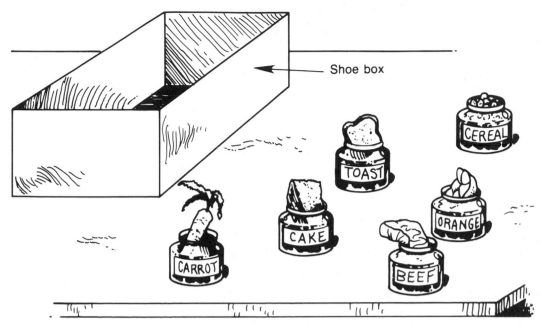

Fig. 7-1. Collect mold spores from different materials. Place them in baby food jars and then in a shoe box to incubate.

Cover the jars with the lids and place them in a box with a lid that prevents light from entering, such as the shoe box. Discard the moldy bread once you have used it to inoculate your food samples.

After three days, evaluate the samples without opening the jars. Determine which food sample grew mold. Are the molds identical? Did the mold grow on all food samples?

Going Further

1. Select the material that grew mold best and see if, in a separate experiment, you can reduce the growth of mold by changing the temperature, the amount of moisture, or the amount of light in which it is stored.

2. Use a material that rapidly produces mold to see if manufactured disinfectants, in measured quantities, will reduce the spread, growth, or changed survival rate of mold. Test which one works best.

PROJECT 2
They're In The Air, Everywhere

Overview

Spores from molds become airborne. Indoor spores become airborne as they dry out. Therefore, if you are allergic to mold, keep moisture in the air to reduce the spread of mold in your house. Dry heat and winter conditions tend to assist mold spores in becoming airborne. Airborne spores can be gathered as they accumulate on surfaces, especially around areas where condensation has formed, such as toilet tanks, window sills, and along the strip on a refrigerator door.

Can we identify mold spores and, in fact, grow them in controlled situations? Can we gather them outdoors? Can we gather them indoors? Is there more mold outdoors or indoors? Is there more mold in the morning or at night?

Materials

- cellophane tape
- 8½" by 11" pieces of cardboard
- magnifying lens or microscope
- thin pieces of plastic

Procedure

Set out six, four- or five-inch pieces of tape, one for each piece of cardboard. Tape each piece with the sticky side facing up across a piece of cardboard (see Fig. 7-2).

In the morning, set one piece outdoors, one near your house, and one indoors. Be sure to mark each of them for location and time of day. After three hours, gather them up and cover them with cellophane to keep out other materials.

In the evening, about three hours before sundown, place the other three boards in the same locations. Remember to mark each one. Just before dark, gather them up.

Using a magnifying glass, determine which piece of tape has the most spores. Conclude whether your hypothesis was right.

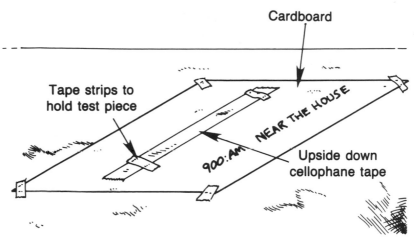

Fig. 7-2. Construct six cardboard structures such as the one shown here.

Going Further

Attempt to grow the spores that you gathered. Rather than cover them, put the cardboard in a container with a piece of bread that has not been treated with preservatives and see if mold grows on the bread. How will you be able to determine if mold was not already on the bread? Use a control? Are there color differences in the molds that grow?

PROJECT 3
Snails Like It
(Adult Supervision Required)

Overview

Algae is a simple plant containing no true roots, stems, or leaves. It does photosynthesize, that is, use sunlight and chlorophyll with water and carbon dioxide to make simple sugars.

Algae grows in fish tanks. Snails are placed in fish tanks to eat the algae. Can we grow algae in a test tube? Will it be a nutrient? Test for sugars and starch. (Caution: Do not eat algae. Just because animals can eat it does not mean people can eat it.)

Materials

- small house plant that will grow from a clipping (such as an African violet)
- test tube or small bottle
- test tube holder or glove
- nutrient solution
- diluted iodine (caution: iodine is a poison—use adult supervision)
- Benedict solution (can be purchased from scientific supply store)
- paper towel or paper filter (such as coffee filters)
- small pot
- stove

Procedure

Grow a plant clipping in a nutrient solution in the sunlight. Algae will form in the solution, creating a green substance in the liquid. After several days, observe the increase in the green substance. Remove the plant. Filter the green substance out of the water, using a paper towel or paper filter.

Test for the presence of starch. Put a drop of iodine on the material and another drop on the paper towel (or filter) to see if it also responds. A change in color indicates the presence of starch.

To test for the presence of sugar, boil the liquid (adult supervision advised) and several drops of Benedict solution. Use a test tube holder or heat glove (see Fig. 7-3). Observe any change in color in the sample that would indicate the presence of sugar. Write your observations on a data sheet. Conclude whether your hypothesis was correct.

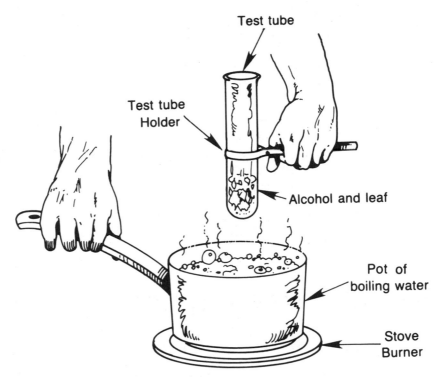

Test tube

Test tube Holder

Alcohol and leaf

Pot of boiling water

Stove Burner

Fig. 7-3. Use tongs for added safety.

Going Further

1. Will algae grow in a higher concentration of salt?

2. If the concentration of nitrogen in the nutrient solution is changed, will the growth of algae increase or decrease?

3. Will trace amounts of copper sulphate ($CuSO_4$) reduce the growth of algae while not affecting the growth of plants?

4. Does the algae use up the nutrients used to feed the plant? How can we test?

PROJECT 4
Friends Forever
(Adult Supervision Required)

Overview

Some organisms live together with other organisms. As they help, they are also being helped. This relationship is called symbiosis. Lichens are not one type of organism, but two. Lichens are both fungi and algae. The fungi provide the moisture and water that the algae need. The algae provides the food that the fungi needs. Living in harmony, they prosper. Without one, the other would surely die.

In this experiment, we investigate how lichens respond to air pollution.

Materials

- several lichens
- clear, large plastic food bags
- candle
- splint or small piece of wood
- match
- atomizer or thoroughly clean spray bottle

Procedure

Locate several lichens growing on trees or rocks. Remove the rocks or tree parts that the lichens are growing on. In order to keep them alive, mist spray them with water daily.

Use two lichens in this experiment, one as the experimental plant and one as the control plant. With an adult present, light the candle. Let it burn well then blow it out. Collect the smoke in a clear plastic bag (see Fig. 7-4) and seal it. To get another type of air pollution, have an adult light a splint or other small piece of wood, blow it out, and collect the smoke in a bag.

Place a bag of air pollution over the experimental plant for an hour or so each day. A new bag of pollution will be needed each day. After several weeks, observe any differences between the experimental plant and the control plant.

Going Further

Locate lichen near a heavily traveled road. You must also find lichen that is not near a heavily traveled road to use as a control. It is very dangerous to try to place exhaust from a car directly into a plastic bag for experimentation and we advise against doing it. Observe any differences.

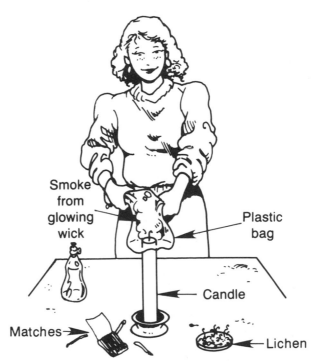

Fig. 7-4. Collect the smoke in a plastic bag and place over the lichens for several hours.

8

Plant Dispersal

Plants are found all over the face of the earth. How can they be so widespread? There are several ways that plants can be transported.

The most basic dispersal is caused by gravity. Many seeds are heavier than air and fall to the ground, usually not far from the parent plant.

Lighter seeds are carried farther from the parent plant by wind. Wind velocity and duration affects the distance traveled by the seeds. Pollen can become airborne and travel thousands of miles in the upper atmosphere. In fact, pollen from widely scattered regions of the earth have been identified. Pollen studies have been done with core borings in the arctic circle. Prevailing winds and updraft regions have a direct effect on plants dispersed by the wind.

Water can also transport plant seeds over great distances. Islands can be populated by mainland plants. Seeds must be strong and thick enough, however, to survive long periods in water. Floods can carry topsoil containing seeds to new areas. Storm erosion water run-offs can also carry seeds. Different species can travel from one place to another by water currents, streams, ocean currents, and even by storm drains in cities.

Animals carry seeds inadvertently. Seeds become caught in their fur, or they use seeds when building nests. Some animals bury seeds. Others eat fruit passing the seeds intact through their digestive system and grow far from the parent plant.

Long ago, people carried seeds from Europe to the New World. Today, however, there are strong laws about bringing vegetation into the country because it might contain insects and diseases. Transporting topsoil carries whole plants to new areas. John Chapman, better known as Johnny Appleseed, carried seeds into new territories.

Some plants shoot out their seeds. Other plants, such as strawberries, send out runners or underground rhizomes (root-like stems) into ever increasing areas.

Some plants reproduce by making bulbs. If one plant has one bulb, the following season there will be two plants, each with a bulb, side by side.

In the tropics, orchids might produce as many as four million seeds per flower. Each orchid flower, however, does not produce four million new plants. The conditions where the new plant finds itself must be acceptable or the plant will not grow to maturity and reproduce. Planters continue to look for new crops with which to make a profit. Oceans, snowcapped mountains, deserts, and other areas with extreme environments might have unsuitable conditions for growth. Favorable conditions for orchids are very complex and limited. Consequently, only a few dozen of the four million seeds might grow.

Finally, seeds can come to earth from outer space! This is merely a topic for thought, but when moon rocks where brought back to earth by astronauts, they were decontaminated to make sure that no organisms (from outer space) were arriving on earth.

Some seeds are protected by fruits or by strong outer coverings. Some seeds are unprotected such as the conifer seed.

Some plants live only one season. These are called "annuals." They must grow and reproduce to prepare for the next generation before they die. Other plants grow in a two-year period, usually not reproducing until the second year. These are called "biannuals." A third group of plants grow from year to year. These are called "perennials." A plant's environment has a lot to do with how it produces seeds.

Is it possible to measure the distances that seeds travel?

This chapter deals with the different mechanisms of plant dispersal, which allows continuation of the species. The seed is the new organism waiting to grow. Where it finds itself and how it gets there is the topic of this chapter.

PROJECT 1
Do Seeds Bounce Or Roll?

Overview

Some seeds bounce when they fall, and others roll, depending on their shape. Try to consider rolling an orange compared to rolling a banana. How much does rolling or bouncing affect the distance a seed is dispersed? Does the ground that the seed lands on help determine how it will be dispersed?

Materials

- several different kinds of nuts (from the super market)
- tape measure

Procedure

Separate the different types of nuts into groups and identify them. Drop them from different heights. Determine if they bounce, and if so, about how high. Does the bounce create a greater distance from the drop point than if it did not bounce. Use 10 or more of each type of nut. Measure each of the drops from the point at which it hit and to the point at which it came to rest. This will include both bouncing and rolling. Do this on several different surfaces. Maintain a data sheet to record your information. Conclude whether some seeds get further from the parent plant than others?

Going Further

Consider the size of the canopy layer for the species of nut you use. Add the radius of the canopy to the distance bounced from the drop. Make a chart.

Fig. 8-1. Drop seeds from different heights and determine how far they travel after they hit the ground.

PROJECT 2
Drop Zone

Overview

As you discovered in the last project, gravity affects seed dispersal. Nuts fall. Apples with seeds inside fall. All seeds fall. Some seeds are so light that they seem to float in the air. Other seeds are wing-like and travel a greater distance because of their shape. Do seeds that seem to float travel farther than wing-shaped seeds?

Materials

- many different species of natural, air-traveling seeds
- small envelopes
- anemometer to measure the wind speed (see the drawing in Fig. 8-2)
- meter, yard stick, or tape measure
- tree or plant identification book

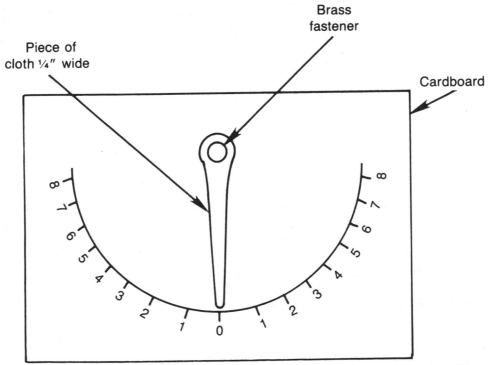

Fig. 8-2. Make an anemometer to measure wind speed for the *Drop Zone* project.

Procedure

Gather and identify as many different air-traveling seeds as possible. Put three or four of each into an envelope. Be careful not to crush or disturb their natural shape. Create a log like the one shown in Fig. 8-3 to identify and log each of the species you have.

Go to an elevated place, a front or back porch, or an open yard or field with a step stool. Measure the wind speed and record it in the log.

Release one seed of each species from the same height. Measure the distance from the release point to the final resting place. For some, the measurement may be in paces. Later, convert paces to meters.

On the next clear day, make a second release and record wind, speed, and distance traveled. Again, on a third day, log the wind speed and the travel distance of each seed. Determine from your results if your hypothesis is correct.

Date	Seed species	Wind speed	Distance
	Maple #1		
	Maple #2		
	Maple #3		
	Dandelion #1		
	Dandelion #2		
	Dandelion #3		
	Milkweed #1		
	Milkweed #2		
	Milkweed #3		
	Pine seed #1		
	Pine seed #2		
	Pine seed #3		

Fig. 8-3. Sample log for recording *Drop Zone* data.

Going Further

1. Are some species only released from trees or plants when the winds are high? If this is true, does it cause them to travel further than they would if the wind were calm? How much wind is needed to release the seeds?

2. Are air-carried seed plants taller than other plants nearby? Do they release their seeds at a later time in the season when other taller plants have died down?

3. An open field that has been left fallow will begin to grow seeds arriving on the prevailing winds. Which species are upwind from the field?

PROJECT 3
Berry Good

Overview

Holly trees are evergreens. They have leaves all year long. There are male and female holly trees. The female holly tree produces red berries. Holly berries are poisonous to humans (although many birds eat them as a part of their diet). **Do not eat them.** The dispersal of holly trees is as wide as the range of the birds that eat them. A bird eats the berry gaining the nutrient from the fruit, but passes the seed through the digestive tract and excretes it. Therefore, in order to determine the extent of seed travel by this method, you must first identify the birds eating the holly berry. How far can the holly seeds be carried? Hypothesize the distance.

Materials

- binoculars
- several bird identification books
- log to record data
- nearby female holly tree for observation

Procedure

Select a female holly tree for observation. The most convenient would be one that can be observed from a window of your home. A tree with more berries will attract more birds. Observe and log the number and species of birds eating the berries. After two weeks, look up the range of the identified birds. Wait two weeks and again observe birds that eat the berries. Using the results from your gathered data, determine whether the hypothesis was correct.

Going Further

How many young holly trees are around a solitary female? The male tree must not be too far away. Draw a map and locate a young tree by distance and direction (and age if possible). Will the direction or openness of a nearby area have any effect?

Fig. 8-4. Birds can carry seeds over great distances, far from a parent plant.

PROJECT 4
Set Sail

Overview

Specific gravity is the term used to compare the weight of a certain volume of one substance to an equal volume of water. If the substance weighs less than water, it will float. If it weighs more than water, it will sink.

Seeds have been known to travel vast distances from one island to another. Atolls and emerging or uplifting islands have many types of vegetation growing in an area where an island hadn't even existed. How did they get there? Some were airborne and others floated. Will seeds native to your area float? If so, for what length of time? While in a stream or river, float time determines the distance traveled.

Materials

- acorns and other local seeds
- 2 large bowls or other containers

Fig. 8-5. Seeds that fall from trees can land in streams and depending on how long they can float, travel far from the parent plant.

Procedure

Gather seeds and identify them. Examine them for any flawed seed coats. If any contain larva or other organisms, discard them. If the seed is merely cracked or slightly opened, however, set it aside to make up a group labeled "Group A." All other seeds should be examined for any differences—maturity, size, etc. . . . Note any differences. These differences might later help you to form hypothesis such as "Greener acorns will float longer than dark brown acorns." Put all complete seeds into "Group B." Set up a log chart like the one shown in Fig. 8-6.

Place the seeds in water at room temperature. Use two containers, one for seeds from Group A and one from Group B. Be sure to maintain the water level to allow for evaporation. Observe how high the seeds float and log your observations. Each day for several weeks, observe which seeds are still floating. Stir after each observation to completely wet seeds. Record all data. Determine from the results whether your hypothesis was correct.

Group "A"

Seed species	Characteristics	Float time	Float height	Sink date
Pin oak	Light green ½" split			

Fig. 8-6. Sample log for recording *Set Sail* data.

Going Further

1. Obtain a map of a local lake or pond in your community. Find out the direction of the prevailing wind at a time when seeds are prevalent. Determine the "start" side of a body of water. Use the map and wind direction to establish a probable "landing" side. Go there and check for species on the "start side."
2. Long-term project: Plant new species of floaters by a pond on the upwind side. In several years, investigate to see if there has been any seed dispersal to the opposite side.
3. Set seeds afloat that have been marked with fingernail polish. Go downstream to check for them. Log the distance and time traveled.

PROJECT 5
Sinking pH
(Adult Supervision Required)

Overview

The pH of a solution indicates the amount of acidity or alkalinity of the solution. A pH of seven is considered neutral, neither alkaline nor acidic. As the pH number decreases, the solution is said to be more acidic. As the pH increases, the solution is said to be more alkaline. Each number on the pH scale is a factor of 10. A lower pH might cause the seed coat to break down faster because of the acid. In this case, if a seed breaks through its coat it would need to immediately be in soil for the seed to grow. Consequently, seeds might not travel as far in low pH streams. Dispersal distance and seed numbers might be reduced.

Materials

- 15 acorns (similar in size and age)
- 15 bean seeds (similar in size and age)
- 10 small containers (200 to 300 milliliters)
- distilled water
- pH indicator (litmus paper, pH meter, or test kit)
- pH increase solution (or potash to raise pH)
- pH decrease solution (or sulfuric acid to lower pH)
- masking tape
- measuring cup

WARNING: Dilute sulfuric acid before using. Use adult supervision because it can burn skin.

Procedure

Set up 10 containers with labels on them. Label two containers "pH 5." Label two more "pH 6." Label the rest "pH 7," "pH 8," and "pH 9." This makes two identical sets. Add the letter A to one set of containers and mark the letter B on the second set of labels. The A is for acorns, which will be put in the A containers. Beans will be put in the B containers.

Next, put two inches of distilled water in each container. Using a commercial pH decrease solution (or potash), mix to obtain a pH of 5 in the containers marked pH 5. Mix each container to reflect the pH number on the label, using pH up or pH down solutions to reach the desired pH level of the water. Number 7 will be plain distilled water.

Place three bean seeds in each B container and three acorns in each A container. Observation is a key factor in this experiment. Make observations morning and night for several weeks. Record all of your data, as shown in the chart in Fig. 8-7. Using your results, determine if your hypothesis was correct.

Going Further

1. Grow the seedlings using the solutions. Do they prefer a particular pH?

2. How long can seedlings be kept alive if they are left in the solutions? Add sunlight. Increase the quantities of seeds. Remove several every two days after they have sprouted in order to grow them. Hypothesize the period of time it will take when they will not be able to grow.

Date	Group A pH 5 AM|PM	Group A pH 6 AM|PM	Group A pH 7 AM|PM	Group A pH 8 AM|PM	Group A pH 9 AM|PM	Group B pH 5 AM|PM	Group B pH 6 AM|PM	Group B pH 7 AM|PM	Group B pH 8 AM|PM	Group B pH 9 AM|PM

Fig. 8-7. Sample log for recording *Sinking pH* data.

PROJECT 6
Turn Me Loose
(Adult Supervision Required)

Overview

The seed of a conifer is locked in. It is trapped unless the cone opens. Some cones do not open unless they are subjected to heat. Therefore, they do not open and release seeds without a forest fire. One species of pine that requires a high temperature to release seeds is the lodgepole pine. How will dormancy or freezing change the requirement for high heat? How much heat is needed? Must the cone catch fire? How does the seed survive the fire? Does the cone burn poorly and stop burning? Do the seeds fly off in the heat updrafts? Hypothesize about the temperature and conditions.

Materials

- 16 cones from a species requiring heat to release seeds (such as the lodgepole pine)
- oven
- cookie sheet (moist blotter paper)
- dark and warm growing area
- clock or watch
- tongs, oven mitten, or pot holder

Procedure

Using adult supervision, preheat the oven to 250 degrees. Set four cones on a cookie sheet and place them in the oven. After two minutes, remove one cone. It will be very hot so use tongs or heat gloves! After four minutes, remove another cone. Similarly, remove one after six and one after eight minutes. Observe the cones to see if the seeds are free. If they are, attempt to germinate them.

Do the same procedure at 225 degrees, 200 degrees, and 275 degrees. You might have to make adjustments for increasing time and temperature. Set up a chart like the one shown in Fig. 8-8 to record observations and results. Study the results to determine if your hypothesis was correct.

Temperature	2 Minutes	4 Minutes	6 Minutes	8 Minutes
200 Degrees				
225 Degrees				
250 Degrees				
275 Degrees				
300 Degrees				

Fig. 8-8 Sample log for recording *Turn Me Loose* data.

Going Further

1. Will high temperatures help other conifers? Test several species for cone opening and seed dispersal. Will the seeds germinate?

2. Do the seeds need dormancy when they are loose? Do they need freezing? Set up conditions and test.

Sources

This resource list is compiled to give you a mail order source for seeds and other botany supplies. Each address has been checked for accuracy.

Seeds

Crosman Seed Corp.
P.O. Box 110
East Rochester, NY 14445
716-586-1928
Vegetable and flower seeds.

Gleckler's Seedman
Metamora, Ohio 43540
Large selection of standard and unusual vegetable seeds.

Landreth Seed Co.
P.O. Box 6426
180-188 W. Ostend Street
Baltimore, MD 21230
Has been selling vegetable and flower seeds for 200 years. Big selection. Available by the packet, ounce, and quarter-pound.

Mellinger's Garden Catalog
2310 W. South Range Rd.
North Lima, Ohio 44452-9731
Sells mail order seeds, bulbs, plants, hydroponic plant food, and gardening supplies such as small netted peat pods for seed germination.

Stokes Seeds Inc.
Box 548
Buffalo, NY 14240-0548
Catalog extensive vegetable and flower seeds.

Chemicals and Nutrient Solutions

Carolina Biological Supply Company
2700 York Road
Burlington, North Carolina 27215
1-800-547-1733
Mail order firm selling complete line of laboratory supplies, hydroponic study kits, and chemicals.

Eco Enterprises
2821 N.E. 55th St.
Seattle, WA 98105
1-800-426-6937

Mail order firm selling complete line of nutrient solutions, individual chemicals, growing containers, indoor lights, and equipment such as pumps and timers.

Peters Fertilizers
Grace Horticultural Products
62 Whittemore Avenue
Cambridge, MA 02140
Source for standard fertilizers, nutrient solutions, perlite, and vermiculite growing mediums.

Equipment

Edmund Scientific Company
101 E. Gloucester Pike
Barrington, NJ 08007
609-573-6250
Free catalog available. A good source for lab equipment such as test tubes, motors, and pumps.

Fisher Scientific
4901 W. LeMoyne St.
Chicago, IL 60651
1-800-621-4769
Laboratory apparatus, chemicals, water test kits, and hydroponic experiment kits.

Frey Scientific Company
905 Hickory Lane
Mansfield, OH 44905
1-800-225-FREY
Laboratory apparatus, chemicals, water test kits, and hydroponic experiment kits.

Hydro-Gardens, Inc.
P.O. Box 9707
Colorado Springs, CO 80932
303-495-2266
Equipment for those who are actively engaged in growing plants and/or produce for resale or research. Special low nutrient solutions for

tomatoes, cucumbers, and lettuce which growers can add for desired nitrogen. Equipment such as bag culture growing systems, top spray automatic growing systems, and other commercial scale watering systems available.

Science Kit & Boreal Laboratories
777 East Park Drive
Tonawanda, NY 14150-6782
1-800-828-7777
> Laboratory supplies, terrariums, hydroponic starter kits.

Sargent-Welch Scientific Company
7300 North Linder Ave.
P.O. Box 1026
Skokie, Ill 60077
312-677-0600
> Laboratory supplies and hydroponic starter kits.

Greenhouses

Texas Greenhouse Company
2701 St. Louis Avenue
Fort Worth, Texas 76110
817-926-5447
> Greenhouses for residential and commercial use.

Magazines, Newsletters, Leaflets

Flower & Garden (The Home Gardening Magazine)
P.O. Box 5962
Kansas City, Missouri 64111-9983
> Published bimonthly. Subscription $8 per year.

Horticulture Magazine
P.O. Box 51455
Boulder, CO 80321-1455

Hydroponic Society of America
P.O. Box 6067
Concord, CA 94524
> Nonprofit organization that promotes and encourages national interest in scientific research in hydroponics by sponsoring meetings and disseminating knowledge through various types of publications. Bimonthly newsletter *The Hydroponic/Soil-less Grower*. Membership dues $25 per year.

Hydroponics As A Hobby

Leaflet number 423. Available from Rutgers University Extension Service, Dennisville Road, Cape May Court House, NJ 08210. An interesting and informative 16-page leaflet featuring an overview of hydro-ponics. Fee is $1.

Nutriculture Systems: Growing Plants Without Soil

Station bulletin number 44. Department of Horticulture, Agricultural Experiment Station at Purdue University, Media Distribution Center, 301 S. 2nd Street, Lafayette, IN 47905-1092.

Organic Gardening

Emmaus, PA 18099-0003

For the backyard gardener. Includes articles on gardening and health.

The Avant Gardener Newsletter

238 East 82nd St.

New York, NY 10028.

Eight-page monthly newsletter by Horticultural Data Processors. Subscription $15 per year. News and tips for gardening enthusiasts.

Additional and more detailed information can be found by checking with the following sources.

1. United States Department of Interior Office of Public Affairs, Room 7211, Washington, DC 20240

2. United States Department of Agriculture, Office of Public Affairs, Room 402-A, Washington, DC 20250

3. Smithsonian Institution, 1000 Jefferson Drive S.W. Washington, DC 20560

4. Botanical Gardens (federal, state, county, local)

5. Parks (federal, state, county, local)

6. Reserves (federal, state, county, local)

7. Museums (federal, state, county, local)

8. Forest Services (federal, state, county, local)

9. Special interest groups, such as garden clubs (national, state, local)

10. School clubs

11. Colleges and universities

12. Libraries: Use libraries to identify experts and their addresses. Also use the reference book *Reader's Guide to Periodical Publications*.

Glossary

algae—A simple plant containing no roots, stems, or leaves. It is the green material found in ponds or unchlorinated swimming pools.

asexual—Reproduction with only one parent. For example, growing an African violet plant from a leaf clipping.

Benedict's solution—A prepared solution used to determine the presence of sugar.

botany The scientific study of the plant kingdom.

canopy layer—The leaf mass at the top of trees that create a layer of sun-absorbing material.

capillary action—Water molecules that adhere to each other. Capillary action in plants cause water and nutrients to travel up the tubes in a plant.

catalyst—A substance that assists a chemical reaction.

chlorophyll—A green substance that acts as a catalyst, in the production of food during photosynthesis in green plants.

control group—When doing experiments, a control group is the group that has all the variables maintained. For example, if you want to test the effects of carbon monoxide on plants, you must have two equally healthy plants. Both plants would receive exactly the same care and conditions (soil, sunlight, water). The experimental plant, would receive additional carbon monoxide. The other plant would be the control plant. The control plant receives maintained conditions while the experimental plant receives the variation.

corm—A thick rounded underground stem base and buds that act as reproductive structure, such as a crocus or gladioli.

cotyledon—The storage area in a seed for growth during germinates.

deciduous—A broad-leafed hardwood tree, such as an oak tree. Characterized by leaves that fall off at the end of a period of growth.

experiment—A planned way to test a hypothesis.

Fresnel lens—A lens that concentrates light.

fungus—A simple organism that does not produce its own food as plants do. Some scientists do not consider fungus to be in the plant kingdom.

geoponics—Plants grown in soil.

germinate—The period of time it takes for a seed to develop roots, stems, and leaves.

herbicide—A substance used to destroy unwanted plants.

hydroponics—A method in which plants are grown without soil. Plants are grown in a nutrient solution, sometimes with a soil-less medium to provide physical support such as sand, which provides no nutritional value to the plant.

hypothesis—A theory or educated guess. "I think when asked how much they would weigh on Mars, more boys will have accurate guesses than girls."

leech—To run water slowly through soil and dissolve out nutrients.

lichen—A symbiotic organism combining algae and fungi. The algae helps the fungi and the fungi helps the algae.

observation—Looking carefully.

parasites—Plants that receive nourishment from another plant but do not give any benefit to the host plant.

percolated—To drain liquid through a porous medium.

perlite—Porous pebbles, or rock. Because perlite has no nutritional value to plants, it is used in hydroponics as a growing medium.

petiole—The area between the leaf and the stem of a plant.

pH—Potential hydrogen. pH is measured on a scale of 1 to 14 which indicates the acidity (sourness) or alkalinity (sweetness) of water or soil. A pH of 7 is neutral. Each number on the scale is a factor of 10 from the next value. Water with a pH of 5 is 10 times more acidic than water that has a pH of 6. Adding potash to water that is too acidic or adding sulfuric acid to water that is too alkaline, brings the pH closer to neutral.

phloem—Miniature tubes that transport food through a plant.

photosynthesis—The process green plants use to produce food by sunlight.

pollination—The movement of pollen grains from the stamen to the pistil of a flower. These organs can be on the same flower or on a different one. When a pollen grain unites with a seed located in the pistil, an embryo develops.

quantify—To measure.

rhizome—An underground stem like a root.

sample size—The number of items being tested. The larger the sample size, the more significant the results. Using only two plants to test a hypothesis that sugar added to water results in better growth would not yield a lot of confidence in the results. One plant might grow better simply because some plants just grow better than others.

saprophytes—Plants that receive nourishment from dead or living organisms.

scientific method—A step-by-step logical process for investigation. A problem is stated, a hypothesis is formed, an experiment is set up, data is gathered, and a conclusion is reached about the hypothesis based on the data gathered.

symbiosis—A relationship between two organisms living together in harmony. Lichens, for example, are both fungi and algae. The fungi provides the moisture and the water that the algae need. The algae provides the food that the fungi needs.

species—A biological classification.

stomata—The opening in the bottom of a leaf where it takes in carbon dioxide.

terrestrial plants—Plants that are grown in the ground opposed to plants grown in water hydroponically, or that naturally grow in lakes and oceans.

transport—The movement of materials (water, waste, minerals, oxygen) throughout a plant.

tropisms—A plants responses to various stimulation. Chemotropism is the response to chemicals. Geotropism is the response to gravity. Hydrotropism is the response to water. Phototropism is the response to light. Thermotropism is the response to heat. Thigmotropism is the response to touch.

tuber—A stem that grows beneath the ground, such as a potato or fern.

turgor—The stiffness or firmness of a plant caused by water in plant cells.

understory—The plant growth, low bush shrubs, and other vegetation that grows above the ground but underneath tall trees whose high branches and leaves form a canopy layer. The three layers from top to bottom are canopy layer, understory, and ground cover.

vascular—Plants that have vessels like miniature tubes or straws which transport food and wastes.

vegetative propagation—Producing new plants from the parts (roots, stems, leaves) of an existing plant. A whole new African violet plant can be grown by cutting a leaf and putting it in water. Roots and other leaves will soon begin to grow. Vegetative propagation includes cutting, grafting, and budding.

vermiculite—A naturally occurring mineral that contains millions of tiny cells, trapping air and water. It has no nutritional value to plants and is often used in hydroponics as a growing medium for physical plant support.

xygote—The beginning of a new organism in seed reproduction.

xylem—Miniature tubes that transport wastes through a plant.

Index

salt, 61
  seasonal growth and, 65
  soil compaction, 53
  water additives and chemicals and,
    44
  water tests for, 42
hydroponicum, 50
hydrotropism, 73

_____ I _____
infrared light, photosynthesis and, 29
isolating plants, effects of, 91, 93

_____ L _____
leaves
  position of, 36
  surface area of, 100
lichens, 111, 118
limitations, 4

_____ M _____
magazines, newsletters, leaflets, 142
maple syrup (sap), 106
models, 3
molds, 112
  spores of, 114
monocotyledon, 96
mosses, 111

_____ N _____
nutrients, 80, 140
  changing levels of, 56
nutrient transport projects, 95-110
  capillary action, 109
  colored water, 96
  leaf surface and, 100
  life cycle of, 102
  maturing and ripening, 102
  phloem identification, 108
  saps and sugars, 106
  transpiration, 98
  xylem identification, 104

_____ O _____
oil spills (see also pollution), 69

_____ P _____
parasites, 118
perennials, 122
pH factor, 42, 43
  common vegetables, 43
phloem, 108
photosynthesis experiments, 23-39,
  95, 100
  amount of light affects, 24
  carbon dioxide amounts, 38

chlorophyll and, 31
  hydroponics and, 67
  leaf position and, 36
  plant respiration and, 33
  plants that do not use, 111
  starches and sugars, 27
  type of light affects, 29
phototropism, 73, 75
plant dispersal experiments, 121-138
  drop zone, 125
  fire as means of, 136
  holly berries and birds, 128
  pH factor and germination, 133
  seed movement, 123
  water borne seeds, 130
planting depth, 8
pollution, 69, 118
  air pollution, 33, 118
  oil spills, 69
  water pollution, 69
protozoa, 111

_____ Q _____
quarantine, 121

_____ R _____
reproduction projects, 7-22, 121
  dormancy periods, 20
  planting depth, 8
  soaking seeds, 17
  soil types, 15
  temperature effects, 11
respiration, 33, 95
root systems
  chemotropism and, 80
  hydroponics vs. geoponics, 63

_____ S _____
salinity, 61
sample size, 2
saps and sugars, 106
science projects, 1-6
  assumptions, 2
  competition, 5
  conclusions, 1
  demonstrations, 3
  experimentation, 1
  hypothesis, 1
  individual vs. group, 3
  judging projects, 4
  precautions, 4
  problem statement of, 1
  topic selection for, 3
seasonal growth, 65
seeds (see also germination), 140

animal dispersal of, 128
  dispersal of, 121
  drop zone for, 125
  fire required by some, 136
  movement of, 123
  pH factor affecting germination, 133
  production of, 102
  soaking seeds, 17
  water borne, 130
sexual reproduction, 7
soil compaction, 53
soil types, germination affected by, 15
starches, 27, 116
stimulation projects, 73-94
  black walnut herbicides, 78
  chemotropism and roots, 80
  geotropism, 82
  grouping and isolation, 91
  no-stimulus environment, 93
  phototropism, 75
  sounds, 89
  thermotropism, 85
  thigmotropism (touch), 87
stomata, 33
sugars, 27, 106, 116
symbiotic relationships, 118

_____ T _____
temperatures, germination rate and,
  11
thermotropism, 73, 85
thigmotropism, 73, 87
transpiration, 95, 98
tropism, 73

_____ U _____
ultraviolet light, photosynthesis and,
  29

_____ V _____
viruses, 111

_____ W _____
water pollution, 69

_____ X _____
xylem, 95
  identification of, 104

_____ Z _____
zygotes, 7